"Phuc Luu powerfully presents a Christian foresight of holistic healing communities for the traumatized, the unanswerably suffering, and the brokenhearted from sin, sickness, racism, impoverishment, and war. Although Luu came to the United States at the age of four, he reverberates a collective memory of the effect of the Vietnam War and of unresolvable wounds of that tragedy, providing an Eastern vision of Jesus' message. A moving, thought-provoking, and transformative book for all suffering people."

—**ANDREW SUNG PARK**, professor of theology and ethics at United Theological Seminary and author of *Triune Atonement*

"Phuc Luu writes between multiple worlds of citizenship, nationality, ethnicity, and God's kingdom. The richness of his testimony reroots us into our bodies and reminds us of God's incarnation. Capturing Jesus' invitation to move out of 'othering' and into presence, Luu drives home that Christianity is not meant to be a spiritual exercise alone. In *Jesus of the East*, Luu pulls on the strands of secular gnosticism found in Cartesian thought, and weaves the text with personal stories and holy narratives, revealing the deep woundedness in humanity and God's intentional liberation. From the misty mountains of Vietnam to the fog of culture, we are pulled by this brilliant text to make space for our own emerging narrative of beautiful rebirth."

—**C. ANDREW DOYLE**, Episcopal bishop of Texas and author of *Citizen: Faithful Discipleship in a Partisan World*

"Phuc Luu has written an insightful, provocative study that challenges many of the presuppositions of dominant theology among us. Luu judges that Western theology offers a misguided, distorted vision of God and of humanity. Informed by insights from Korean Minjung theology and the powerful restorative work of *han*, Phuc Luu sees that the gospel is not about pardon from sin but about restoration of the wounded. This in turn leads to a focus on the human body, not the soul, and especially on the bodies of the broken and wounded, whom God restores and permits to grow fully into God's own image. The outcome is a deeply different theology that assigns very different work to God and that affirms a very different prospect for humanity. In the grip of Constantine and Descartes, we in the West have so much to unlearn and so much to learn afresh from the Asian church. What we may learn afresh is indeed good news for us all, and for the church as a carrier of that good news."

—WALTER BRUEGGEMANN, professor emeritus of Old Testament at Columbia Theological Seminary

"While reading *Jesus of the East*, I was swept away on an incredible theological journey where the author, Phuc Luu, integrated deep research and thought, woven together with his personal narrative, creating a compassionate theology as inspiring, skillful, and accessible as a great work of art or a grand poem. Such a gift is rare in the field of theology. I am thankful for the opportunity to be exposed to such a hopeful and helpful book, and you will be too!"

—RANDY WOODLEY, distinguished professor of faith and culture at Portland Seminary of George Fox University and author of *Shalom and the Community of Creation*

JESUS OF THE EAST

JESUS OF THE EAST

Reclaiming the Gospel for the Wounded

foreword by **GREGORY BOYLE**

PHUC LUU

한

HERALD PRESS

P R E S S

Harrisonburg, Virginia

Herald Press
PO Box 866, Harrisonburg, Virginia 22803
www.HeraldPress.com

Library of Congress Cataloging-in-Publication Data
Names: Luu, Phuc, author.
Title: Jesus of the East : reclaiming the gospel for the wounded / Phuc
  Luu.
Description: Harrisonburg, Virginia : Herald Press, [2020] | Includes
  bibliographical references.
Identifiers: LCCN 2019059959 (print) | LCCN 2019059960 (ebook) | ISBN
  9781513806716 (paperback) | ISBN 9781513806723 (hardcover) | ISBN
  9781513806730 (ebook)
Subjects: LCSH: Jesus Christ--Biography--History and criticism. | Jesus
  Christ--Political and social views. | Christianity--Controversial
  literature. | Church and social problems. | Eastern churches--Doctrines.
Classification: LCC BT301.9 .L78 2020 (print) | LCC BT301.9 (ebook) | DDC
  232--dc23
LC record available at https://lccn.loc.gov/2019059959
LC ebook record available at https://lccn.loc.gov/2019059960

JESUS OF THE EAST
© 2020 by Herald Press, Harrisonburg, Virginia 22803. 800-245-7894.
  All rights reserved.
Library of Congress Control Number: 2019059959
International Standard Book Number: 978-1-5138-0671-6 (paperback);
  978-1-5138-0672-3 (hardcover); 978-1-5138-0673-0 (ebook)
Printed in United States of America
Cover and interior design by Reuben Graham

Unless otherwise noted, Scripture text is quoted, with permission, from the *New Revised Standard Version*, © 1989, Division of Christian Education of the National Council of Churches of Christ in the United States of America.

Scripture quotations marked (CEB) are taken from the *Common English Bible*, copyright 2011. Used by permission. All rights reserved.

Scripture quotations marked (KJV) are taken from the *King James Version* of the Bible.

Scripture quotations marked (NASB) are taken from the *New American Standard Bible*®. Copyright © 1960, 1962, 1963, 1968, 1971, 1972, 1973, 1975, 1977, 1995 by The Lockman Foundation. Used by permission.

Scripture quoted by permission. Quotations designated (NET) are from the NET Bible® copyright © 1996–2018 by Biblical Studies Press, L.L.C. All rights reserved.

Scripture quotations marked (NIV) are taken from the *Holy Bible, New International Version*®, NIV ®. Copyright © 1973, 1978, 1984, 2011 by Biblica, Inc.™ Used by permission of Zondervan. All rights reserved worldwide. www.zondervan.com. The "NIV" and "New International Version" are trademarks registered in the United States Patent and Trademark Office by Biblica, Inc.™

24 23 22 21 20   10 9 8 7 6 5 4 3 2 1

For the women in my life—their strength permeates this work.

CONTENTS

FOREWORD

For thirty-five years, it has been the privilege of my life to walk with gang members in Los Angeles at Homeboy Industries. This work of accompanying the demonized so that the demonizing will stop is a gift beyond my ability to describe.

I got a text yesterday from a homie who has struggled mightily with trauma and mental health issues. "I can't decide if I'm good or bad," he texted. I found myself telling him, "You are unshakably good. You are my son. You just need to heal some things." There are theological notions of God and sin that have failed us and left us malnourished. They have allowed the wounded to see themselves as "less than." The proliferating messages of a colonizing Christianity have not given us real food, but have left us feeling as I do when I catch a homie feeding his toddler Flamin' Hot Cheetos. "Dawg . . . don't give your kids crap."

Good theology, Annie Dillard says, "removes absurdities." *Jesus of the East* is good theology. Phuc Luu reignites our longing to live as though the truth were true. He cuts up our meat for us, with scholarship so complete and personal reflections so tender that we feel nourished and quickened to live differently. This book is so important because it invites us to take seriously what Jesus took seriously: Inclusion. Nonviolence. Unconditional loving-kindness. Compassionate acceptance.

Challenges abound for us in this book, and we realize that we all have embraced a Christianity that has forgotten Jesus. We find here the Christ who inhabits the places of *han*, or unresolved suffering, the Christ of whom Saint Ignatius of Loyola writes, "See Jesus standing in the lowly place." After savoring this book, you will want to stand with the *han*-ridden so that you, too, will welcome your own wounds and commit never to despise the wounded again.

Luu decolonizes our minds, and his challenge to Western Christianity is not shrill, but comforting in the end. He helps us see that sin is not stain but wound. I am writing this during Lent, a time when we are called to repent, which Luu correctly asserts is about moving beyond the mind we have to rethink things. Only then can we be ushered into a newfound sense of restorative and distributive justice and the exquisite mutuality of kinship which is God's dream come true. Mirabai Starr says, "Once you know the God of love, you fire all the other gods." Luu knows the expansive and spacious heart of this God and proceeds to "fire all the other gods" that keep us from seeing our shared humanity, our unshakable goodness, and our longing to love as we are loved, without measure and without regret.

You will feel not just fed, but nourished, by this book. Its theology of the people restores and retrieves the mystical lens of Jesus who sees wholeness and who longs to heal us all still. Our polarizing, divisive times make this book required reading. You will feel invited to stand in the lowly place. Lucky for us, that's where the joy is.

—*Gregory Boyle,*
founder of Homeboy Industries and author of
Barking to the Choir and *Tattoos on the Heart*
Lent, February 2020

INTRODUCTION

The history of Christianity is one of cultural appropriation. The religion of "the Way" was birthed through the vision of a Palestinian Jewish carpenter who ministered primarily to the sick and the oppressed. But three centuries later, in the Western Roman Empire, powerful oppressors adopted the Christian faith, granting it an elevated cultural status. In the hands of Constantine I, Christianity was transformed into a component of political citizenship, and the state-sanctioned church awarded a monopoly on the administration of divine grace. In America, this type of Christianity was marshaled to justify the oppression of enslaved people, a heavily redacted version of Christianity that demanded servitude and obedience from the enslaved. But enslaved Africans in America reappropriated Christianity as a religion of hope that offered escape, not in a world to come, but through literal freedom from bondage in the here and now. Today, Christianity must be reappropriated again by reclaiming it from the clutches of theological traditions that have perpetuated the victimization of people, our bodies, the land, and the relationships around us. The Christian faith must be returned to the people to whom it rightfully belongs and for whom it was intended—those who are wounded and who have been sinned against.

Jesus of the East is a guidebook for those seeking to wrestle the historic faith of Christianity back from a tradition shaped by oppressors. This work of reclaiming the Christian faith draws on the historic tradition found in Eastern Christianity, which focuses on the liberation of people rather than on God's punishment for original sin. It also draws on Minjung theology, an indigenous Korean theology developed by and for the common people that focuses on the need to remedy *han*, or intense woundedness. This book is not an apologetic for Eastern Orthodoxy, or for any other denomination, but rather an argument for a way of reimagining theology around Jesus.[1]

Perhaps today more than ever, this is where the focus of theology should be placed. In our #MeToo, #BlackLivesMatter, immigrant-fearing world, Christians must abandon the faith of the conquerors and colonizers and return to a faith that brings healing to the hurting, and wholeness where damage has been inflicted by oppressive forms of Christianity. These forms of oppressive religion have condoned the presence of sexual predators among the clergy while also seeking to claim the moral high ground by advocating for unborn fetuses. They have refused to ordain women and LGBTQ+ people but have supported men who abuse their power in relationships with women, persons of color, and persons who do not identify in sexually binary or heteronormative ways. They seek to proclaim the "truth" of Christianity, but are easily given to false narratives, "alternative facts," the denial of scientific evidence, and blatant and continual lies.

We are approaching a breaking point in our religious dialogue. With the turn to secularism and the separation of church from state during the nineteenth century, some religious institutions came to fear the loss of Christianity's influence. However, the demise of Christianity may come not from an increasingly secular world, but from the type of Christianity that presently exists. Perhaps a better question than *whether* Christianity will survive in today's age is the question of *which kind* of Christianity and *whose* Jesus will be passed down to our theological descendants.

Many in the West feel disdain for Jesus—not the Jesus who reflects the ideals of American life, confirms our cherished beliefs, and does not oppose our ways of living and believing. Rather, they feel contempt for Jesus the Palestinian Jew and itinerant teacher who healed the sick and preached a message of resistance against the political and religious status quo of his day. Their contempt is for the one who lived among the poor and outcast and criticized the established religious order for demonizing and segregating the most vulnerable and those in need. Their contempt is for the Jesus whose life is marked by sorrow, pain, poverty, empathy, and struggle against the forces of this world. This Jesus has become a scourge to our existence and a scapegoat on whom to pour out our fear and hurts. This Jesus is difficult to follow because he does not provide practical advice, such as guidance for finances or family life; he is not a teacher of Christian self-help or systematized theology. He is the rabbi of the oppressed and shunned, the physician of the uninsured, the liberator of the incarcerated—a living, breathing, hurting person whose life and thinking are foreign to much of Christianity in the West.

Yet I cannot help but see this Jesus among us, among the poor and disenfranchised, among the outcasts and wounded. I see him in the acts of kindness, empathy, and forgiveness that occur when people grapple with their own brokenness and seek also to provide healing for others. I have seen this Jesus in our communities and have witnessed the ways in which he brings healing to our divisions, how his vision for humanity helps us to see ourselves, each other, and the world differently, and how he offers the ability to sustain this form of existence. This Jesus provides a promised peace beyond the mere cessation of conflict, a peace that is summed up in the word *shalom*, meaning "well-being" or "welfare." But this Jesus of the poor is entirely strange to many of us in the West because in our Western culture, an alternative form of Jesus—a Jesus who came to save sinners but who has abandoned the sinned-against— has won out in the contest to define Christian faith.

In an episode of the Canadian sitcom *Kim's Convenience*, Mr. Kim and his son, Jung, are not on speaking terms because of a familial conflict that began when Jung was convicted of a crime and subsequently dropped out of high school. Jung has since become an assistant manager at a car rental service, where he is a spokesperson for a campaign to recruit more ethnically diverse employees for his company. The company has produced life-sized cardboard cutouts of Jung to advertise this new marketing strategy, and Mr. Kim comes across one of these cutouts on the sidewalk. Although initially taken aback by his son's image, Mr. Kim decides to alter this image to advertise the products of his own convenience store. When neighborhood children vandalize the cutout, Mr. Kim is forced to repair "Jung," turning him into a cardboard Frankenstein held together by duct tape. Regrettably, Mr. Kim's relationship to the cardboard likeness of Jung is more tender than the one he has with his own son. Eventually, the cardboard-imitation Jung falls into a state of disrepair and Mr. Kim is forced to abandon it in a dumpster.

We in the West have inherited a cardboard cutout of Jesus, a thin fabrication rather than the living Jesus of history and the Gospels. This Jesus has emerged victorious in the struggle to define Christianity and has been written into both the history and the theology of Western culture. Many will eventually see that the Jesus of the West is a flimsy imitation, a prop for ideas that do not hold up to scrutiny, and will toss this imitation Jesus aside. But what will serve as a replacement when this imitation Jesus is abandoned?

In order to describe the "Jesus of the East," I first need to tell the story of how the "Jesus of the West" came to be, and why the

Jesus of the West provides only a lifeless semblance of the historical Jesus. I will outline the ways in which the Jesus of the West is *already* the reigning champion in Western culture, and will examine some of the theological propositions and most cherished beliefs of Western Christianity that have been accepted as theological truth. Many of these ideas are still debated in academic circles, but where they have been put into practice, in the arena of the church and the public square, they are now largely unchallenged. We will see how the Jesus of the West is an imitation Jesus taped together by complex and sometimes convoluted theological doctrines that seldom encompass the real life and teachings of Jesus, much less the reality of living in this world.

The ubiquitous call within evangelical churches is for sinners to accept Jesus and be forgiven. This is also plain to see in most Western Christian traditions. The Book of Common Prayer used in the Episcopal Church features prayers for the forgiveness of sin: "Almighty God have mercy on you, forgive you all your sins."[2] Our worship, prayers, and theology have all been shaped around an image of a Jesus whose primary mission is to save sinners.

In contrast to the Western church, the Eastern church fathers primarily held a view of Jesus not as someone who staved off God's wrath, but as a healer of humanity who brought people back into divine communion with God. They portrayed Jesus as a mediator who turns humans toward God through revealing God's faithful and enduring goodness, rather than as a sacrifice offered to turn God back toward humans. According to the Eastern fathers, God never gave up on or became angry at humanity. It was always the other way around: humanity was ashamed of its own acts of distrust and violence, and as a result turned away from intimacy with a tender and loving God. Yet God never abandoned humanity, and even joined humanity in our greatest experiences of pain and shame.

The reconciliatory and restorative aspects of Eastern theology share commonalities with Korean Minjung theology. Minjung theology had its genesis in the identification of the oppressed Korean people with the suffering of Jesus and with the people to whom he ministered, literally "the crowd" (Greek *ochlos*). In the Gospels, the crowd are the common people whom Jesus addressed, came to be with, and served, and to whom he brought healing. The experience of woundedness in Minjung theology is encapsulated in the unique word *han*, or "unresolved suffering." As we examine the life of Jesus, we will see how *han* emerged in his life and in the lives of those around him. The concept of *han* will help us ground our view of Jesus in real-world concerns, rather than in myths, fictions, or ideas created for the sake of theological gymnastics.

In chapter 1, I outline Western visions of the kingdom and Jesus and demonstrate how these visions serve the purposes of those in power rather than those of the people Jesus came to serve. Chapter 2 explores the idea that the Western Jesus is supported by a mind-body dualism that originated in gnostic thought and is still taught today, prompted by the legacy of Enlightenment thinker René Descartes. Chapter 3 outlines the mission of Jesus, who sought to holistically heal the wounds of the oppressed, rather than provide an otherworldly escape. In this chapter, I will demonstrate how the enfleshment of God ultimately united humanity and God.

Chapter 4 explores the resistance to Jesus' mission, a resistance rooted in a system of scarcity that sought to both enslave people and turn them into commodities for trade, and to deny their identities as divine image bearers. In chapter 5, I argue that scarcity is ingrained in our Western theology of the cross, which is based on the belief that God had to make a sacrifice of God's Son in order to redeem humanity. In contrast, the vulnerability and abundance of God's love provide an alternative vision to the system of scarcity. The incarnational suffering God is the balm that heals the damage and brokenness brought on because of death. In chapter 6, I explore how Jesus' life overcomes death, which is the consequence of and not punishment for hurtful actions. Lastly, in chapter 7, I describe a truly just and renewed world and relate stories of restored humanity that emerges when we see Jesus of the East in our midst.

I came to these convictions not in one torrent of revelation, but through a gradual intellectual and spiritual journey that started in high school and continues today. Profound crises of faith and thought led me to difficult conclusions about God and this world, but also to important texts and ideas that cleared my path. After reading an intriguing work by the Jesuit theologian Bernard Lonergan on "the intelligibility of redemption," I concluded that the cross might not be an absolute necessity to accomplish the mission of God in the world.[3] Even though God used the cross as an instrumental means to help humanity face our violent way of "othering" people, an unbalanced fixation on the cross neglects the crucial events of the incarnation and the victory over the cross that occurred in the resurrection. My research led me to several conversations with Methodist theologian Andrew Sung Park on the profound sociological subject of *han*. It was this concept of woundedness and the idea of sin as "sickness" that led me back to the Eastern fathers, and especially to Irenaeus of Lyons. I was also directed to this path by many conversations with the Canadian theologian and patristic scholar Bradley Jersak.

In entering any classroom, church, or speaking venue, I am mindful that peoples' cherished beliefs are precious to them, even when they may be incorrect, because those beliefs form the foundation of their view of the world. Some may experience a challenge to these beliefs as a personal violation, an assault on private space. I wish to enter this conversation with respect and humility. What I am asking is not that you, my reader, change your mind, but that you consider these ideas as a possible way out of our current dilemma.

There are deep divisions among the peoples of this land, divisions that have grown out of a history of woundedness that we have not even begun to address. No matter which political party controls our nation, no matter how much we "put God back" in our schools, no matter how much we pray, we will not find healing until we treat the sickness that afflicts us and not just its symptoms. I ask that you consider the ideas in this book. Try them on, as you might a new sweater, and see if they fit with your experiences of the world and life. I ask that you imagine with me the possibilities of what can be.

I hope that, through these pages, Christians will see Jesus with new eyes and therefore become co-creators of a world that dispels the myths of the past, fully embracing the *euangelion*, or good news. Just as Jesus in the first century sought, through his work and preaching, to correct the prevailing perspective of who God was for his time, so Jesus of the East serves as a corrective for our religious attitudes and beliefs. Theology, doctrines, and religious beliefs are not static. Despite what some think, they are not written in stone, but are written on the heart (Romans 2:15; 10:9). Theology, literally "conversation with God," evolves and grows through discussion and debate, but many Christians have inherited stagnant doctrines from the church and have continued in and contributed to systems of injustice, misogyny, racism, and violence. Because these interpretations remain dominant and seem to work for many, they have rarely been challenged outside academic circles. If these doctrines and beliefs are not replaced, they will continue to perpetuate the wounds of our society and our world.

In whatever way you come to this book, may we have a conversation in which you and I acknowledge each other's humanity and the image of the divine in each other. We are all fallible, and our ways of seeing are partial and imperfect. My desire is that we come to the table with this in mind, and with hope and compassion for one another.

Minjung
민중신학

People's theology—*ochlos*, ὄχλος (Greek), crowds, multitude, people, those to whom Jesus ministered, the sick, the poor, the prostitutes, the tax collectors, the shunned, the oppressed, the sinned-against. Emerged from the experience of Christians in South Korea.

1

VISION

For it is impossible for anyone to heal the sick, if one has no knowledge of the disease of the patients.

—IRENAEUS OF LYONS, *Libros quinque adversus haereses*

In the parched Judean desert, somewhere near the Dead Sea and Jordan River, a lone Palestinian Jewish man dwells, seeking to confront his personal demons. His face, caked with a mixture of dirt and sweat, is as cracked and parched as the ground. The birds of prey sweep around him and loiter in the shadows of the shrubs, waiting to see if he will become carrion. Along with the small animals that scurry about, they provide uneasy company, their sounds the only ones he hears except for the breath of an occasional breeze that offers respite from the scorching heat.

The ascetic Essenes also inhabit these harsh lands, where they have sought retreat from the godless world. But Jesus has come to this place to bathe himself in all the temptations the world has to offer. His first temptation is a demand to demonstrate his might by turning the rocks that litter the landscape into food to satiate his own hunger. His stomach groans, his rib cage visible through his thin sienna skin.

In addition to satiating his own hunger, he could also feed the masses. It would be an easy solution for people who are hungry for the bare necessities, people easily swayed by the grandeur and spectacle of "bread and circus." If he would translate his power to turn stones to bread into commensurate political power, he could do so much good—but at the same time, so much harm: a grand showman in the political arena of their minds.

Jesus dismisses this temptation, declaring that he feasts only on the eternal truth of God's word.

Yet another vision. Jesus is brought up to the holy temple, the most sacred of places, the center of the universe, the tallest pinnacle in the land. He is confronted by the true test of his faith, a demand that he surrender his life and plunge toward his death. Surely God will catch him. His heroics would prove the world wrong about YHWH's seeming inability to defend Israel, God's people. God's existence would be undeniable. The salvation of the Messiah would also mean the salvation of the kingdom of Israel. Everyone would see the power of YHWH, the LORD almighty, the one who can save all from doom. If he braves this feat, he could show the world in an instant all that God can do—vanquish enemies, provide riches, restore wealth, dispel the doubts of heathens. There would be no more confusion as to which God and which faith was true. All doubt would be erased.

Jesus again dismisses this temptation, pointing out that these proofs of God's power are ultimately empty.

In the shimmering heat, Jesus' eyes behold another vision. He is taken to a high mountain, to a vantage point where he can gaze upon the whole world. Monotonous shifting sand dunes rise to reveal a vision of a world of wealth and prestige, of kingdoms that received their power from the evil one. Like the land of Egypt, these empires have amassed their possessions on the backs of their people. The power of these kingdoms is within his grasp, simply waiting for him to take hold of it, calling him to receive their fame and false promises. He need only keep his might from crumbling, delicate sandcastles slipping through his hands. This temptation is to join in the work of all dictators and despots.

Jesus dismisses this final temptation by declaring that there is only one whom he will serve—not the forces of evil, not the ruler of the kingdoms, but the one who sustains him.

The desert is relentless, reminding him of its vastness in all these possibilities—avenues that he could pursue, but that would lead to disaster for the entire cosmos. Hunger pangs mirror his deep desire. The longer he stays in the desert, the deeper the longing burns into his being—longing to create a new way of life with the world, a new relationship with creation itself. As he looks out into the Judean landscape, he sees a vision of a kingdom built not on the backs of the poor, nor on deals with the wealthy, but formed through restoring broken lives and mending those wounded by the religious and political machinery that plagues them. His calling is to bring together people who can dress the wounds of others while also receiving care for their own wounds. These wounded healers will come to see each other as he sees them, not as tools in a system or as cogs in the machinery, but as a name and face, a person and a story.

By day, the sun beats on his brow as he sits in meditation and prayer, his back hunched over and his head hung low. He becomes an indistinguishable feature of the landscape, like a rock or a shrub. He pores over each word of the Torah as if they were written anew and being read for the first time. He takes them apart and digests them one by one, their meanings transformed as they enter his body, no longer letters on a page but words absorbed into his flesh. Words are kneaded like dough that will be baked in the oven of God's mouth for Jesus to hungrily feed on.

The nights cool the land and allow him to sleep. He dreams of his people. Their faces flash through his mind, their sorrow and their pain. These images fill his heart and head. They give form and structure to his words, stanzas to his poems, paragraphs to his prose. He will craft his message for them, for their ears, a strange message they will hear but not quite decipher until they enter into friendship with him, learn what he has learned, and experience what he has experienced. He will seek the same—to listen and be changed.

And so the desert becomes a place of provision. He witnesses oases springing up after a storm quickly passes, quenching his parched lips. In emptiness he sees life, poured out for him even in the harshest conditions, just as it is provided for the beasts and plants that inhabit the land. Like the people of Israel long ago, he learns abundance in the desert, how to survive in a land that is foreign and prone to the harshest of conditions.

After forty days, he rises from fasting and meditation to begin his work. He sets his sights on the Jordan River, where he will bathe in the history of humanity and quench his thirst in the story of his people. He will be washed as the *ben adam*, the Son of Man, not to condemn humanity for sin but to cleanse them as one disinfects a wound. He will emerge from the waters with them and take them to his new world. His entrance into the stream will be a way to guide them to a different country, another nation. He will carry them into the waters and lead them out into another kingdom, a kingdom built not only by him, but together with them.

Until then, this vision will germinate in his heart. It waits to take root, grow, and flower.

BETWEEN TWO WORLDS

With a squeak of tires, the plane landed on the tarmac at Hà Nội. Forty-four years had passed since my parents and I left our native land of Vietnam. This trip with my wife, her parents, and a handful of friends was my first time back to the place we had fled.

We decided to begin our journey in the north, the region not of my birth but of my ancestry. My father's family had moved south to be a part of a war between brothers and sisters and countries near and far. For some, this war is a long-faded memory, but it still holds much trauma for me and for many others. As writer Viet Thanh Nguyen reflects, "All wars are fought twice, the first time on the battlefield, the second time in memory."[1] Vietnam is a battleground of memories.

Before Saigon fell, we left by plane in the dark of night. Because my father was a lieutenant colonel in the South Vietnamese Army and my mother worked at Trans World Airlines, we had relatively little trouble making it out with the first wave of refugees. Many others were not as fortunate. Some who exited on boats never made it to a safe shore. Vessels were seized by pirates, people were taken into slavery, their bodies used to appease the gods of punishment and suffering. But that was the history of our people, of many conquests, and wars, and of fleeing. I do not know how deeply the war entered my soul as a four-year-old boy. Did the trauma of war leave a mark on me like the bombs that scarred our land, just as my grandfather's imprisonment by the Communist government left an indelible mark on my father? Were the wounds of my parents passed down to me, not like old recipes, but like disgraceful things one hides away, never to be discussed?

But on that day over four decades later, I returned to the land of my ancestors, to the north, where my father and his parents come from. It was not until toward the end of our tour that a bittersweet feeling settled in. I was no longer Vietnamese, but Việt Kiều, a foreigner, a Vietnamese person living abroad, a point made by Vietnamese nationals after they heard my American accent.

"You're Việt Kiều?"

"Yes," I would respond with slight embarrassment.

I am now Vietnamese American. Between two worlds, I am not a citizen of one country, nor am I entirely accepted by the other. In the United States people still ask, "Where are you from?" I respond, "From Houston." But this question is intended to draw attention to my difference, as if we did not share the same love for barbecue brisket, the same excitement when the Astros won the World Series, and the same flooded roads and houses three years in a row.[2]

I am an inbetweener. That is exactly the way that Jesus calls his disciples to live, existing between one vision of the world and another. Jesus was not a patriot of Rome, nor was he a teacher of Jewish orthodoxy. He was crucified for being both a traitor and a blasphemer. Jesus had no allegiance to the empire of Rome or to the earthly Zion. Neither were his home. Rather, he longed to dwell with his people, to live among those who needed him and loved him. He who eternally danced with the Father and Spirit now entered another dance, not with humanity in general, but with specific humans in particular. He became brother and friend, teacher and student, co-conspirator and comrade. He ate with them, laughed and cried with them, struggled with them, and bled with them. Their voice was his. He could not be separated from them. Yet he was always foreign, always a stranger in this world.

This is the reality I face as a person caught between two countries, peoples, and cultures. I am bound to and cannot be torn apart from the place where I live, but I am also constantly viewed as different. Jesus and his followers lived in the same way, as foreigners.

When Christians are unwilling to feel out of place in their culture, they are not really practicing the Christian religion. In building our own "safe spaces" in churches and bookstores, in academia and other institutions, we are only trying to ease our feeling of foreignness by creating a land and culture of our own. By using insider language to separate "us" and "them," we are attempting to anesthetize ourselves to the painful reality that the world in which we are living is *not* ours. We do not own this land. We do not own this world. Notions of dominion are fictions of the mind. The painful reality is that we are all called to live as foreigners.

The belief that we own this land has especially ravaged North American Christianity. The original identity of North American Christians was as pilgrims and refugees, but it became that of colonizers and conquerors of the land. In recognizing that this place truly does not belong to us, many of us face a gnawing and painful reality. Until we have come to the unsettling realization that the prized possessions of land, soil, borders, and boundaries are not solely ours, we will find no liberating comfort. Until we face this reality, those Christians who resist it will fight and tear at whatever they can to keep their impermanent identities intact. This is what drives much of Christian identity in North America—the need to cling to a reality that does not really exist, the myth of a Christian land and a Christian world.

The great gift of life is to exist as a participant in a life and world that is not entirely our own. It is a constant invitation to love what is not our own, and thereby receive the possibility and joy of love returned. We are part of an intricate tapestry of relationships: with others, with the earth, with animals, with the air. We can no more claim ownership of any of it than we can claim ownership of the sun and stars. But many of us are driven to make possessions and people our own, to grasp and grab, just as the Edenic couple took hold of the forbidden fruit despite already having received all the other ripe produce of the garden. In doing so, we fashion forms of government and systems that control and dominate. We live as if this life itself is not enough to satisfy us and meet our needs. We live as if the opportunity to eat and be full, to love and be loved, to know and be known is not enough, as if we need more. We do need all these things in order to survive, but what will come from all our effort?

We live like parents who spend all their time building a life for their children at the expense of living life *with* their children.

Jesus' mission was to liberate people who were caught in oppressive systems and to bring healing to those hurt by them. These systems prevented people from receiving medical care and finding well-being, from thriving and flourishing as persons made in the image and likeness of God. Though the religious systems labeled them "sinner" and "leper," he called them "friend." Though the governmental systems denied them citizenship, he included them as compatriots and sojourners, sisters and brothers. In doing so, he established new ways of being and living that threatened the present order. He called these ways of being the "kingdom of heaven" or "kingdom of God," but the language of kingdom is only an analogy, a word picture painted for comparison. The kingdom that Jesus offers is more than a human kingdom or empire or country. Jesus was not creating the "Christendom of heaven" or the "Christendom of God." "Kinship" and "family of God" come closer to describing his vision, but even the image of family has its pitfalls. In whatever way we name it, Jesus was birthing another way of living.

There were many ways in which Jesus sought to depict the kind of life he intended for those who became part of God's kingdom. Jesus compared the kingdom of heaven to a mustard seed, which begins as a tiny speck but grows until it is large and reaches out, providing a perch for the birds of the air (Matthew 13:31-32). This kingdom is not isolated, but generous and giving. Jesus also compared the kingdom to yeast that a woman folds into flour to leaven bread (v. 33). This yeast does not arrive in packets from the grocer, but is a fungus naturally harvested from the air. When combined with flour and liquid, it causes the dough to ferment and rise. The baker's hands work it in until it permeates the dough, where it consumes sugars and gives off alcohol and carbon dioxide, slowly inflating the dough, lifting it out and up. Yeast strengthens the dough and creates flavor and a perfect blend of textures, causing the baked bread to become crispy on the outside and chewy on the inside. The very yeast that is seen as ritually unclean is the essence of this bread.

Similarly, the kingdom gathers people into a web of relationships, kneading them together until they give rise to something much greater than their isolated components. The organic nature of the kingdom gives it far more endurance than the artificial structures of this world, which crumble and decay all too quickly. All human empires, including the empires of Syria, Assyria, Persia, Babylonia, Rome, Britain, France, Germany, and Japan, eventually fell. Even this experiment that we call the United States of America will eventually be no more, but the relationships that sprout from our natural coming together are ever more resilient.

When Jesus used kingdom language, his followers knew exactly what he intended. His invitation was a call to betray one's country for another. His language implied opposition to the kingdom of Rome and to Caesar, and even to the Herodian kings, the figurehead kings of Israel under Roman rule. Roman law considered Jesus to be an insurrectionist. In the Roman Empire, there was no king other than Caesar, but when Jesus accepted the mantle of messiah, it was a mantle not only of kingship, but also of solidarity with a conquered people. In acknowledging his mission, Jesus, like Moses, betrayed his country. He was executed under the same condemnation that was given to Barabbas, a criminal instigator. Jewish religious law convicted Jesus as a blasphemer, disloyal to Jewish law, one who claimed the same authority as YHWH God. He was sentenced by the Jewish Sanhedrin and then given over to the Roman tetrarch Pontius Pilate to be tried again and executed.

Obedience to religious and state laws was paramount for the Pharisee Paul of Tarsus, whose identity was both Jewish and Roman. This concern is reflected in his instruction to the church at Rome to "let every person be subject to the governing authorities" (Romans

13:1). But Paul, who turned from persecuting the people of the Way and became a spokesperson for this nascent religious group, also nuanced his position. He clarified that "love does no wrong to a neighbor; therefore, love is the fulfilling of the law" (Romans 13:10). Even the laws of government must be subject to the laws of love and hospitality.

Citizenship in God's kingdom differs from the political citizenship of those who belong to a nation. Kingdom citizens may be called to violate their nation's laws in order to fulfill the kingdom law of kinship, compassion, and love. If the New Testament were written today, the term "nation of God" might be used to describe this way of living, not as an endorsement of nationalism, but as mockery of it. Using such a name for the people of God induces Christians to become disloyal citizens to their home nation, to become people who are aware that their citizenship in God's kingdom will conflict at times with the obligations of national citizenship, and are reluctant to pledge allegiance to tribe and country. Kingdom language highlights the tension and forces a confrontation between conflicting loyalties. It raises questions about when one should oppose the law of one's nation to uphold the law of the kingdom of God, which above all calls us to the "law of love."

Kingdom citizens are called to stand up when the laws of the land conflict with the law of love. Kingdom citizens are called to live like Rosa Parks and Martin Luther King Jr. Like Corrie ten Boom, who illegally protected Jews seeking sanctuary from the Nazis, kingdom citizens protect the vulnerable, even when doing so is against the laws of the nation that holds their citizenship. Christians might be called to do many culturally and legally unacceptable things and may even go to prison for the kingdom of God. Kingdom citizens should easily abandon national citizenship when the requirements of their nation are in opposition to their commitments as citizens in God's kingdom.

Christianity began as a persecuted religion practiced by Jews who had broken away from traditional Judaism, and which then expanded to include non-Jews as well. Christianity did not become a national religion until 313 CE, when the Roman emperor Constantine I (272–337 CE) issued the Edict of Milan, transforming a persecuted religion into the state religion of Rome in one fell swoop. Before the conversion of Constantine, Christians were often pacifists and generally did not join the military. Many of the early Eastern fathers, such as Origen of Alexandria (c. 184–c. 253 CE), wrote treatises against military service.[3] They had witnessed or heard reports of the cruelty of the Roman Empire: accounts of the crucifixion of their master and his followers at government hands and of the torturous deaths of fellow Christians beheaded or torn apart by lions. As a result, Christians were wary of the military state. They saw the use of force to take human life as counter to the grain of Jesus' mission in the world.

The early Christians were communal and participated in the sharing and fair distribution of wealth. Christians were egalitarian, treating as equals both enslaved and free persons, women and men, and Gentiles and Jews. In contrast to their cultural counterparts, they sought to be transformed into the likeness of Christ (2 Corinthians 3:18; Romans 8:29) and therefore to be restored to the image and likeness of God (Genesis 1:26). Christians did not see themselves as insiders and others as outsiders, but sought to include others in God's kingdom.

While in prayer and meditation, the apostle Peter, a devout and observant Jew, had a vision of ritually unclean and clean animals (Acts 10:9-16). In this vision, Peter heard a voice that told him to "kill and eat" of these animals. Peter, who replied that he had never done so, was initially perplexed, but later interpreted this vision not simply as instruction about the abolishment of dietary laws, but rather as a revelation that Gentiles should no longer be excluded and viewed by Jews as unclean. God's kingdom is expansive and includes all people as made in the image of God (James 3:9). The religion that began as predominantly for Jews became one of inclusivity and adaptation. This new inclusivity brought increasing suspicion by the Roman government. They allowed the Jewish religion, but would not allow this new religion practiced by people who had been expelled from the synagogue, thereby forfeiting legal protection, and who refused to bend a knee to Caesar.

With Constantine's conversion, the religion of the persecuted, powerless, and disenfranchised rapidly became a religion of the powerful and dominant. Constantine attributed his victory over his rival Maxentius at the Battle of the Milvian Bridge to a vision of the cross in which he heard the words "In hoc signo vinces" (By this sign, conquer). The Jesus who was crucified for being a traitor to his country and a blasphemer of his religion was hailed by Constantine as the force behind the defeat of his own people. The instrument of torture had become a symbol of power and bloody conquest.

Constantine's form of inclusion, brought about through the power of his sword, was a violent one. His vision featured the defeat of Rome's enemies through the cross of Christ. Under Constantine, the message of the cross became a battle cry, and the image of the cross a symbol of victory. In return, Christians were finally safe from harm, but this safety and security came at the cost of their freedom and resulted in the loss of the essential goal of their faith, to liberate humanity.

The difference between the aims of Constantine and those of the kingdom that Jesus preached were subtle but vast. Constantine sought not to enter the kingdom of God, but to build his own Christian kingdom, Christendom. Constantine used Christianity to win wars and conquer his enemies, rather than to resist evil and love his enemies. In doing so, he transformed the Roman culture into a "Christian" culture. Under Constantine's form of Christianity, people did not need to be transformed, but were required to conform to Roman citizenship. Roman citizenship became equated with belonging to the Christian church, with no perception of conflict or tension between the two.

TO SEE THE KINGDOM

John 3:1-10 relates an important exchange between Jesus and Nicodemus, the reluctant disciple who visits Jesus in the dark of night. This is an often-read passage because it contains the phrase "born again," or "born from above," to signify spiritual renewal. But what is more fascinating is the way Jesus responds to comments from Nicodemus, the Pharisee, about his ability to perform "signs."

Jesus tells him, "Very truly, I tell you, no one can see the kingdom of God without being born from above" (v. 3).

After this comment, Nicodemus remarks on the apparent impossibility to being born when one is old. Jesus replies, "Very truly, I tell you, no one can enter the kingdom of God without being born of water and Spirit" (v. 5).

Any reader who blinks will miss the switch in words, from seeing to entering. It is as if Jesus is somehow saying to Nicodemus, to see the kingdom is to be in the kingdom. To envision the life for which he was reaching was to reach for it, even to grasp it. This act of envisioning is integral to the process of being "born from above." It is a type of reimagining.

Many in Jesus' time could neither envision nor grasp the kingdom. They lived like the prisoners in Plato's famous allegory of the cave, where they had been chained with their heads and bodies fixed so that they spent their existence gazing on mere shadows and strange forms, believing them to be real. Their eyes had become too weak to behold the reality and truth of the world outside the dim cavern of their minds. But Jesus understood that reality was about more than mental projections, about more than images cast onto the walls around us through the manipulation of others. Power and privilege are the illusions of people who build empires, who hand out security and safety as tokens in exchange for loyalty and allegiance. Their caves are their empires, constructed with the machinery of conquest and colonialization. Within these empires, people are no longer valued as human beings, but are seen as dispensable commodities or tools for production, valued only for what they can do. The shadows of a hope, a way of life, a dream, are cast before them like shadows on the wall of a cave, a pale semblance of the kingdom of God.

The Judean desert stripped Jesus of everything, forcing him to confront the fragility of his own humanity. He saw reality not in the pure forms of ideals, but in the lives of his people. In seeing reality, he freed himself from the cave of unreality. The desert fathers and mothers of Egypt imitated Jesus' way of life when they retreated from society to enter *hesychasm*, stillness and quietness, as a way of bringing peace to a world filled with striving for wealth and power. Anthony the Great (251–356 CE), known as the father of monasticism, also sought freedom through retreating into the desert for prayer and worship.

Reflecting on Jesus' experience in the desert may lead us to consider the price we pay for our way of life, which often allows us to avoid being stripped bare in the way that Jesus was in the desert. What might we gain if we stilled the constant buzz of our electronic devices and put a halt to the daily demands of our busy lives? The desert to which God calls us may not be a physical place, but can be found in any space that allows us to be stripped of the things that enslave us and make us less than human. This kind of desert calls us to be mindful of who we are and how we relate to others. It enables us to reject the "idols of the heart." These idols include the images and expectations imposed on us by our culture that define how we are expected to live, behave, and see ourselves and this world. They ravage our lives.

Jesus eventually left the silence and emptiness of the desert to return to his people and their difficulties, to a world marked by woundedness. Unlike the Essenes at Qumran, permanent retreat into the desert was not an option for Jesus. Love and suffering go hand in hand. Pain and longing, heartbreak and fear, cannot be distilled from love. Love was as much a part of Jesus as he was a part of creation. The Buddha sought to end suffering by ceasing to desire, but the deep desire that Jesus encountered in the desert led him to find a deeper love. When Jesus retreated alone, he did so in order to reenter the world revived and fulfilled. He was not a hermit removed from problems of the everyday; he fully understood the depths of humanity. Becoming fully flesh meant that Jesus was able to bleed, to cry, to have needs, to depend, to hunger, to thirst, to breathe air, to suckle at the breast of all those who nurtured him. He depended not only on his mother for nourishment, but also on the community in which he lived. Jesus revealed a God who is not lofty, detached, and self-sufficient, but who is open and vulnerable to the possibilities of the world.

Among his people, Jesus envisioned a new world, a new way of living and being. He liberated those who had been "othered" by being labeled as lepers and sinners, prostitutes and cursed, unholy and poor. The holy, elite, and powerful created structures that allowed them to maintain their privileged status through sheer force and violence, and at the expense of those who struggled to carve out a mere subsistence. Fear of punishment and retribution bolstered these structures, and the suffering of many undergirded the happiness of a few; the system had been engineered to work this way for countless centuries.

But these structures were not sustainable. Every empire and government that conquered this land collapsed, washed away like sandcastles—the Assyrians, Babylonians, Greeks, and eventually the mighty Romans. Jesus' vision provided a way of nonviolence and trust. But how could his people see this? He would have to demonstrate it to them through his words and actions, through his ability to pour healing and wholeness into their lives.

The new kinship of Jesus was built one life at a time, one love at a time. It was constructed in pain and sorrow, in heartache and tears. He entrusted his life to his people, and they entrusted theirs to him. Over three decades, these relationships became the foundation of his new world. The more his people saw these connections, the more reality around them changed. Soon they formed an unstoppable movement, one which death could not erase.

WESTERN VISIONS OF JESUS AND THE KINGDOM

To simply speak the name Jesus is not sufficient to encompass a vision of God's mission and kingdom. One must ask, "Whose Jesus?" and "Which Christianity?"[4] Christian history is populated with competing and rival versions of Jesus. If we are to claim to be Jesus followers, specifying which version of Jesus shapes our faith and practice is an important task.

The Jesus depicted by the dominant strains of Western Christianity is not the Jesus that the early church, and especially the early Eastern church, knew and depicted. In recent decades, theologians working from the contexts of liberation, Black, feminist, womanist, and queer theology have tried to recapture the original vision of Jesus' kingdom. Minjung theology, a Korean theology of the people, takes these other theologies into account while also focusing on Jesus' true mission: to heal and bring liberation to those who are wounded and who have been sinned against. Like these other modern theologies, the focus of Minjung theology is on the oppressed, but Minjung theology seeks to locate liberation for the oppressed in the healing of *han*. Together, the Jesus portrayed by the Minjung theology of Korea and by the Jesus of the Eastern church form the "Jesus of the East."

By the fourth century, Christianity had been transformed from a religion of the working class and ostracized into a religion of the king, from the religion of the persecuted to the religion of the persecutor. As a result, the theology of Christianity was reshaped to reflect the politics of its newly adopted parent-state. Theology that sought to bring healing, wholeness, and hope to the sinned-against was transformed into theology focused on the sinner—the one who caused harm. This form of Christianity offered those in power and the Roman government what theologian Dietrich Bonhoeffer would later term "cheap grace." This new Jesus would not suffer the fate of the wounded healer but was held up as the savior of those who devoted their lives to the Roman church and who had been baptized for their sins. In a union of theological and political power, the means of grace was now controlled by both the church and the government.

This Christianity of the powerful remained the religion of the Western world even after the Reformation and remains the dominant form of Christianity in the Americas to this day, and especially in the United States. At times, this Western depiction of Jesus has been subverted by a Jesus who is present among the poor and powerless, those needing healing and liberation, and those Jesus came to serve. The Jesus who can be found among the poor has been held up by brave congregations and individuals who oppose the cult of an angry God and blind nationalism. However, these glimpses of hope are few and far between. It is my intent to place these beside the dominant theological narrative as an alternative story of Jesus. My goal in doing so is not to gain the satisfaction that my ideology, way of reading Scripture, or theological nuances are correct, but rather to provide people hope.

Droves of people, especially young people, are leaving the church, especially evangelical congregations, and many of them see few alternatives. These young people, sometimes called the "nones," now include about 55.8 million people in the United States who have no specified religion.[5] The nones are not necessarily atheists but have changed their religious identification from Christian to "other." Some proclaim, "I'm spiritual, but not religious." Many are sick of a religion that does not fit with their everyday experiences of life.

The faith they have been offered is often not consistent with science, with environmental and social concerns, or with logic and common sense. Many people in this age of technology are not willing to assent to beliefs such as the assertion that there was once a literal garden called Eden where the world's original progenitors were created and where they committed acts that spread sin throughout all humanity. They find themselves unable to assent to the assertion that the world is ten thousand years old, that it experienced a great flood during which representatives of each kind of animal were saved in a giant ship, and which left a handful of human survivors who became the ancestors of every contemporary nation. Simply stated, many people who are Christians find that what some churches and denominations desire them to believe does not make logical sense, while many other explanations outside Christianity do have coherence.

Views of God that are contradictory and inconsistent with Scripture also create a significant barrier to Christian faith for many people. These include the view that God is vindictive and unjust, requiring complete obedience to arbitrary laws, and that this God fails to follow the same laws which God has prescribed for humans. For those who have disobeyed God, this God requires a sacrifice to appease God's wrath; without it, there will be literal hell to pay. Many people who reject God do not reject God per se, but rather an image of God as one who is all powerful yet vindictive in punishing others, including God's only Son. They reject a God who claims to be just but relies on the eternal fires of hell to carry out this justice, inflicting them even on unbaptized infants, starving children, and those who have never heard the "good news of Jesus Christ." They reject a God who is said to be loving and forgiving to the sinner but who abandons those who have been sinned against. This God is two-faced, and many people are clever enough to see through these contradictions and leaps in logic. They are leaving the church in search of more coherence and consistency.

The Western version of Jesus dominated for many centuries because it gave people meaning. It provided salvation from hell and a pathway to heaven. It provided people an acquittal from self-imposed guilt. This Jesus assures us, "You are all right, perfectly fine, even in all your poor reasoning and illogic, in all your contradictions and overlooking of the obvious." Faith in this Jesus is comforting for many of us because it does not challenge the way we live. It does not move us to seek more knowledge about ourselves, the world, and God, and as a result, does not challenge us to expand our love. This faith is often sincere but is very much a reflection of a believer's own culture. Jesus of the West allows us to retreat into our own private beliefs, where our faith will not be challenged by logic or reasoning.

I once was a member of a Baptist church that displayed the Christian flag next to the American flag, and that celebrated the Fourth of July with as much enthusiasm as Christmas. In this church, Christianity was equated with Americanism and vice versa. Reaching the world meant reaching the "lost peoples," usually people of other countries. This congregation did not see people of other countries as God sees them—as God's people—and did not consider how Christ might already be present with them, but rather sought to teach them and convert them in the same way that empires have used Christianity to colonize other cultures for centuries. I've observed a similar pattern in many mission churches that spring up in large cities. Rather than coming to know urban people and their cultures, rather than being a friend and seeing Jesus in them, the people who bring this kind of faith seek to colonize. Their mission is to replicate the mission of the plantation, just as France colonized Vietnam in the nineteenth century. The French first sent the missionaries to convert the Vietnamese, and then, under the guise of protecting their missionaries from persecution, they carved out their own territories in the area that became known as French Indochina.

During the rise of modernization and the Industrial Revolution, which paralleled philosophy's "turn to the subject," in which humans became the center of knowledge, Western readings of the Bible became isolated, privatized, and often literal. Many of the Eastern fathers, such as Origen of Alexandria, had a trifold approach to Bible reading that saw Scripture as having literal, moral, and spiritual meanings. In contrast, many Western churches, especially evangelical ones, teach that a literal interpretation of the Bible must necessarily provide an accurate description of reality (even though, in practice, they may not take everything in the Bible literally). These churches use the mantra "The Bible says it; I believe it; that settles it" to protect the individual Christian from external criticism and thoughtful analysis.

This private and literal reading of Scripture has become the dominant way in which people are encouraged to engage in devotional reading, not recognizing that Jesus read his Bible, the Torah, much differently. For Jesus, the Scriptures were always interpreted in dialogue with the authorities of his time and in community with others, an approach that is reflected in Jesus' words "You have heard that it was said, but I say . . ." Those who follow the Jesus of the West are more likely to draw on the apostle Paul's version of

Christianity when reading the Bible than on Jesus' model of interpreting the Bible in community. In other words, many read Paul's
writings to interpret the Gospels rather than read the Gospels to interpret Paul.[6] There is little support in Jesus' teachings and his use of
parables and stories for a literal reading of the Hebrew Bible. When
we gather and engage in dialogue about the text, hopefully we will
begin to see how these discussions expand our perspective to give
us a greater understanding of the Scriptures. Our private, individual lenses become enlarged in order for us to perceive the divine.

Most of the religious people of Jesus' world did not comprehend
who Jesus was or his mission to bring about a new imagination about
the world. They did not recognize God's presence among them even
though Jesus performed miracles, cast out demons, healed the sick,
and raised the dead. As a result, they did not realize that this was
what God was doing in the world. Their preconceived ideas of who
their messiah was supposed to be clouded their ability to see what
was happening right before their eyes. If our perceptions are clouded by individualism and privatized religion, their senses were hin-
dered by a faulty tradition of reading the Law and the Prophets, the
teachings of the Hebrew Bible. They hoped for political and economic security and sought someone who could provide that. The
Pharisees could not find Jesus in their sacred texts. The Sadducees
could not see him in the temple sacrifices. The Essenes did not find
in him their "Teacher of Righteousness" who would be identified by
way of retreating into the desert and abandoning the trappings of
society. These people were religious in their own ways and seem to
have been entirely lost in their own notions. What was in front of
them did not match what they were taught and believed about who
the messiah would be, how he was to rescue them, and for whom
he was coming.

My point is not only about reading the Bible correctly; conservative and progressive Christians can spar endlessly about the right

reading of Scripture. My point is about how we might come to see the Jesus about whom the New Testament actually speaks, the Jesus who is alive and well among "the least of these" in our world. If we try to mold God into something that our minds can hold, what kind of God would that be? Augustine wrote, "If you think you have grasped God, it is not God you have grasped."[7] By this he meant that if we think we have truly figured God out, then it must not have been God we were seeking to understand to begin with. Instead, we have created a God who fits our mental cookie cutters.

Am I falling into these same pitfalls and making my own mistakes in trying to describe the "Jesus of the East"? It is possible. I know that my vision is incomplete, and my eyes are also dull. I "see through a glass, darkly," as the apostle Paul writes (1 Corinthians 13:12 KJV). This is why I am pointing to the Eastern version of Jesus, so that others may see for themselves and "taste and see that the LORD is good" (Psalm 34:8). My role, like that of a Pointer dog, is to direct others, albeit with stories and commentary. It is the job of the reader to follow the direction that I point.

The only way out of this mental quandary may be to begin with real experience of God in the world, to begin in the places where God *really* exists and breathes and has God's being, in the lives of people with whom God came to dwell. We may need to begin with God's presence with the victims of sin, the wounded, with those whom Korean American theologian Andrew Sung Park calls the *han*-ridden. This is where Jesus is doing the work of healing, in flesh and blood, in the reality of life, with the sick and with those in need of a physician.

If we can see this Jesus, or even imagine this Jesus, we will be able to find ourselves with him, living in his story and seeing our stories wrapped up in his. But if, at the outset, we have rejected this Jesus, the Jesus we see will be purely a product of our imaginations, only a myth. We will remain the same persons, our minds untransformed, our countenances untransfigured. We will be comforted with pithy sayings and Bible verses taken out of context, but the gnawing pain will remain, even if it only comes from the faint recollection of a kingdom that is here and a kingdom that could be.

The Man in the High Castle, a novel by Philip K. Dick, paints the picture of an alternative dystopia in which the Japanese Empire and the Third Reich win World War II and the United States is divided between the Pacific States of Japan and the Nazi-controlled Eastern United States.[8] Peace is upheld by the power of heavy-handed governments and by fear. The ovens of Auschwitz have been moved to the States (which are no longer united), where the white ashes of those who were handicapped and mentally disabled still float and fall from overhead. A mysterious book called *The Grasshopper Lies Heavy* provides hope for those who seek to resist the domination of empire. This banned book tells of an alternative reality in which the United States won the war and went on to abolish Jim Crow laws in the 1950s, outlawing racism. Although *The Grasshopper Lies Heavy* outstretches even our present reality, it offers possibility and hope to some of the characters by providing a vision of the world as it could be.

During the early nineteenth century, white enslavers understood the power of the biblical text and its vision all too well. When some of the same people who brought enslaved Africans to the Americas also wanted to "Christianize" them, they gave them a special form of the Bible that had been printed in Britain especially for enslaved people in the Caribbean. This Bible was produced with whole chapters and verses edited out, including verses such as "There is neither Jew nor Greek, there is neither bond nor free, there is neither male nor female: for ye are all one in Christ Jesus" (Galatians 3:28 KJV). The Exodus story of the enslavement of the Hebrews in Egypt and their liberation by Moses was also missing from this book. It did include verses that affirmed the status quo, such as "Servants be obedient to them that are your masters" (Ephesians 6:5 KJV). Approximately 90 percent of the Hebrew Bible and 50 percent of the New Testament were missing from this slave Bible, as if the publisher had not considered the ethics of blatantly producing a redacted version of a sacred text.[9]

These enslaved people were given a Jesus of the West who was not interested in liberation, but in subservience and appeasing their enslavers. Many did not receive the true message of the good news until abolitionist Christians brought them another gospel. Even then, talk about freedom was coded in church services in the form of African American spirituals. Spirituals such as "Steal Away (to Jesus)" and "Swing Low, Sweet Chariot" were freedom anthems, serving to signal that the coast was clear, and giving instruction about how to find the Underground Railroad. Worship included both praise in response to hope and instructions for finding real liberation. This theology was not pie-in-the-sky, but offered a real means of escaping hardship, torture, and cruelty. The liberating power of Jesus of the East had become manifest in the lives of those who were brought and bought into captivity.

———

In Đà Nẵng, I arranged to meet with my uncle, my mother's brother. He picked me and my wife up in his small red coupe, zipped us around the crowded streets, and drove us past a bridge in an area on the river Hàn where a military petroleum depot had once stood. My father had been responsible for the management of that important utility station. As we drove past the bridge, now embellished with multicolored lights, my uncle pointed to something that was not there, a story, a ghost of things past, as if in naming it, it would become true.

My uncle had served as a pilot for the South Vietnamese Army, and his own stories of war were harder for him to tell. The bridges in Đà Nẵng are the symbols of Vietnamese progress. They signal the future, but their dazzling lights do not hide the history of pain. Rather, they illuminate the reality that something is missing.

We live in a redacted world, as if something good of both the past and the present has been erased or marked out by a black Sharpie, as if there is something we are not supposed to see. It is an alternative vision of both what could be and what is. As a Việt Kiều, an inbetweener, I will tell the story of those things left untold.

Việt Kiều

粤侨

An inbetweener, foreign-born Vietnamese, part of the diaspora after the Vietnam War (the American War) ended in 1975. There are 4.5 million "overseas Vietnamese," or "Vietnamese sojourners," who sought political and economic asylum.

2

BIRTH, BEGINNINGS, AND THE BODY

If confession is the cry of the sinner, then lament is the cry of the victim.

—**RUTH C. DUCK,** "Hospitality to Victims: A Challenge for Christian Worship"

For the first time, he opens his eyes to gaze on a new world. And for the first time, unfamiliar smells strike his nostrils, an assault on the senses. And the hunger, the deep hunger. The experience of depending on another being is like nothing he's experienced before. He fusses and squirms and cries. He suckles at his mother's breast and feels the intimacy of her flesh on his. Knowing about this intimacy and living it are two different things.

And *not* knowing, the experience of having chosen to become emptied of all knowledge, is yet another experience for him. To empty oneself out, like a full glass poured onto the ground, is a gift both to himself and to the world. To empty oneself is to lose all in order to gain all, to open one's hands to the world and grasp what one can with one's small fingers, just as his small hands hold on to Mary's dark, fibrous hair.

This is the beginning of his world. Looking up, he is no longer godlike, but fully childlike. The deities of his life are two people— Mary and Joseph—and a community who will feed and clothe him, teach him and nurture him, help form him into the being he will become. Even when he masters speech and has his own thoughts and insights, he understands that he is connected to family and friends. This understanding is woven into his being, part of his flesh, his existence. Their blood is his. Their histories are his. And as he moves into the world, their destinies are also tied to his.

I AM A BODY

It is difficult for me to imagine a life or identity outside of my body. I realize that my body has changed as I have grown up and grown older, and my mind has also changed. I would like to think that I've become wiser, or at least more experienced. My knowledge of the world has matured. I've acquired new skills and abilities. All these changes have come through my body, not apart from it. This awareness of life in my body is not without great difficulty. As a Vietnamese, growing up in Morgantown, West Virginia; Miami, Florida; and Akron, Ohio, I quickly became aware that my body was different from other bodies around me, that I stuck out in the crowd. Even in a diverse city like Houston, Texas, where I've spent most of my life, there are places and pockets of people where the particularities of who I am become apparent not only to me, but also to others around me. This feeling of otherness often results not only from my own feelings of being different but also from many subtle interactions and attitudes that I sense from others.

Many people in the United States respond to differences in other people in ways that are uncommon in other countries. If a white person travels to Asia or Africa, they will likely be received with friendliness, welcome, and a sense of novelty. When I visited South Asia with some white American friends, locals were eager to snap photos of them, like little children seeing real-life unicorns, perhaps because seeing white people in the media had fostered fantastic beliefs about all white people. As a professor in Kenya, I was very well-respected, and my race was never brought up or discussed. People were more interested in life in the United States than in me as an Asian American. But this is often not the case when many citizens in the United States encounter people from other countries, cultures, and ethnicities. The strangeness of difference becomes a cause for discomfort, distrust, fear, and even hatred. This fear manifests in the social construct we call "race." Although it is a social creation, the concept of race has become realized in the history and culture of the United States, and as a result it must be acknowledged as real before we can begin to tear it down. Sociologists Michael Emerson and Christian Smith have called this fixation on race the "racialization" of America.[1]

The U.S. census includes questions and categories about race, not only to determine representation, but also to demarcate the boundaries between people groups. Currently, the census lists five racial categories: White; Black or African American; American Indian or Alaska Native; Asian; and Native Hawaiian or Other Pacific Islander. Interestingly, these descriptions do not refer to essentials, but only to origins and appearances. The Census Bureau defines white as "a person having origins in any of the original peoples of Europe, the Middle East, or North Africa," and Black or African American as "a person having origins in any of the Black racial groups of Africa."[2]

Although most Black people in the United States have some European ancestry, Americans call a person "Black" if that person *appears* to be of African ancestry. Why do we not call a person "white" if their mother was of Irish descent and their father was from Kenya? We do not call such a person "white" because most people in the United States neither see them nor treat them as such. In this culture, white bodies are valued, and Black bodies are devalued. Black bodies are seen and valued not as persons but as tools, perhaps most highly so in sports.

In a recent study of white medical students and residents, over half the respondents indicated a belief that Black people feel less pain and have thicker skin than white people.[3] Educated professionals who have studied biology and physiology believe this nonsense and treat Black patients as if they were less sensitive to pain than their white counterparts. Doctors who hold this belief cannot understand the suffering of their African American patients. An inability to recognize a person as capable of suffering pain is an inability to see that person as human.

These racialized attitudes are compounded by the myth of "colorblindness," which attempts to skirt the issue of race by claiming that color does not matter. Claiming "I don't see race" is only another way of saying "There is no problem with race." Someone once observed that race seems to be very important to me. In a way it is, because race affects and infects almost everything that happens in the United States.

Racism is a constant stain on America. Author Jim Wallis calls it "America's original sin."[4] By "original sin," Wallis means that inequity according to race is a founding principle for this country, one that "still lingers" in this nation, in the criminal justice system, and throughout our culture. This sin has been passed down from generation to generation and must be confronted, named, and treated. We cannot deny its existence. Colorblindness is not an antidote to the problem of racism because colorblindness asks us to remain blind to the reality of a system that allows some to advance at the expense of others, who must stay behind. Colorblindness invites us to refuse to see the problem of racism because seeing it is too difficult. But refusing to see racism is akin to ignoring a tumor while wishing it would simply disappear.

The problem of race is the problem of how we view and treat the body. This problem results from an ingrained modern philosophy that views the body as distinct from the mind, and from a religious heritage that has, by and large, treated the body as foreign and distinct from the soul or spirit. This problem is evident in the history of the treatment of bodies:

- The forced relocation of the bodies of Native American and First Nations people
- The use of African bodies as tools of industrialization
- The treatment of Asian bodies as tools of Western expansion
- The use of Central and South American bodies as tools for agricultural development and building construction
- The scapegoating of Asian American bodies during World War II through relocation and detention
- The scapegoating of Vietnamese bodies for the purposes of unjustified war and the fear of communism
- The scapegoating of African American bodies through the prison industrial complex
- The scapegoating of Middle Eastern bodies for the purposes of unjustified war and the fear of terrorism
- The sexual objectification of women's bodies by men
- The sexual abuse of children's bodies, especially within religious institutions
- The neglect of LGBTQ+ bodies in relation to matters of health and preference

- The neglect and abuse of Black bodies in matters of public health
- The detention of the bodies of asylum seekers from Central and South America
- The commodification of bodies of other species to the extent that they suffer extinction or near extinction
- The exploitation of planet Earth for its resources and the abuse of land

This list is nowhere near exhaustive, but it gives a glimpse of the primary ways in which we relate to one another as bodies. It is through this tender flesh that we relate to one another. We know each other in our bodies before we have fully gained conscious awareness of who we are. In these bodies, we reach out to our mothers to grasp and suckle. In these bodies, we express our deepest yearnings through noises and sounds. In these bodies, some form value systems that privilege some bodies over others.

Early Christian thinkers were adamant about telling the story of God's enfleshment. Theologians often use the term *incarnation* (Latin *carne*: flesh), but this term has often become abstracted in order for the body of Jesus to be used as a tool for salvation, as in the theology of Anselm of Canterbury (1033/34–1109). Anselm argued that the primary reason God became human was to die in order to restore God's honor.[5] But the enfleshment of God was more than just a way for God to save humanity; it was a way that God *joined* humanity. The Eastern church father Athanasius (c. 298–373), borrowing from his predecessor Irenaeus (c. 120–c. 200), summarized the meaning of God's enfleshment in this majestic and often-recited way: "The Word of God became human so that humans can become more like God."[6] The incarnation united God and humanity so that the two could (re)enter into an eternal dance.

This intermingling of the divine and the human was difficult for some Greek and Egyptian philosophies that made a point of rejecting the flesh, and instead exalted the purity of ideas. Gnosticism, a term that comes from the Greek word *gnosis*, meaning knowledge, was an ancient philosophical movement that viewed the flesh with suspicion. Gnosticism was a scourge in early Christianity and has reared its ugly head in many forms of Western Christianity.

Some recent Christian authors have popularized the notion that the dualism between spirit and matter in Gnosticism reflects a dualism between Hebrew and Greek thought of the Bible. I would argue along different lines. Greek thought in the school of Plato and Socrates did point toward "ideals" and did value form over matter. However, Plato's preoccupation with immaterial "forms" did not deny the value of the material world. Socrates simply highlighted the fact that our senses often deceive us and can be an unreliable source of knowledge.[7] Aristotle, a student of Plato, taught that all substances consist of a composite of matter and form. For Aristotle, the human being is an integration of soul (the animating principle of life) and flesh (the material cause of human beings), and not a purely spiritual being trapped in a fleshly cage.

The Gnostics believed that the material world, including the flesh, was inherently evil. They saw bodies as corruptible and prone to decay. The bodies of people, plants, and animals die and are no more. In contrast, Gnostics believed that thoughts and ideas are eternal because they can be passed down from generation to generation and do not cease to be. Gnostics believed that the pursuit of knowledge offers an escape from the flesh, and the more specialized the knowledge, the better. The Gnostics pursued secret knowledge to obtain salvation from the flesh through enlightenment of the soul.

The Gospels, particularly John, provide an outright attack on Gnostic thought. The fourth gospel begins, "In the beginning was the Word [Greek *logos*: logic, notion, rationale] and the Word was with God" (John 1:1). John writes that this *logos* "became flesh and lived among us" (v. 14). The story of Jesus' birth, his genealogy as told by both Matthew and Luke, and his bodily resurrection all narrate an account of the divine nature that did not find the flesh problematic, but rather took it on as integral to the being of the *logos*. The divide between the Creator and the creation became blurred in the enfleshment of God in Jesus. In becoming us, God crossed borders and boundaries to join us. God did not need to save us from the flesh, but restored our flesh, bringing it to divine light.

Gnosticism has important ethical implications. Those who consider flesh to be evil relate to the flesh in one of two extreme ways. They either deny the flesh, as ascetics do, literally whipping it into submission, or lavishly indulge it through decadence, sexual lavishness, and violence, accompanied by extreme denial, skepticism, and isolationism. The gnostic approach to the body is either feast or famine. We can also see the influence of gnosticism in what we call materialism, which is the antithesis of gnosticism and involves the rejection of the spiritual and an overemphasis on the flesh. In one form or another, for centuries, gnostic philosophy has plagued many religions.

The proper attitude toward the flesh and material world was a point of difficulty for the early Christians. As Christianity moved from its birthplace, Jerusalem, this nascent religion became infused with other ideas. Some of these ideas helped give Christianity a fuller expression, and some challenged its core principles. In the region south of Jerusalem and into North Africa, Christianity developed a way of reading the Bible known as the spiritual reading of Scripture, which considered the meaning of Scripture not only literally but also morally and spiritually. The spiritual interpretation of Scripture had its benefit in showing the varieties of Bible reading that are possible. However, this method also opened the way for an overly spiritualized gnostic version of the gospel. Many of the texts that were influenced by Gnosticism can be found in the Nag Hammadi library in Egypt. The spread of gnostic versions of Jesus was especially prevalent. Several non-canonical gospels, such as the Gospel of Thomas, the Secret Book according to John, and the Gospel of Judas were written by Gnostic Christians.[8]

Farther north in Asia Minor (present-day Turkey), a philosophy called Docetism emerged which proposed that Jesus simply appeared to be a human being. This was a dispute against the doctrine of the incarnation, about whether God could suffer and be put to death. The reasoning was, if Jesus had both a divine and human nature, then God must have died on the cross, and how could God die? The conclusion was that the body on the cross could not really have been God, and that Jesus only appeared to have died on the cross. Docetism was a spin-off from Gnostic ideas. For Docetic thinkers, God's suffering was beyond comprehension, as it perhaps is for many contemporary Christians in the West. Those who suffer must undergo change, and many stubbornly refuse to believe that the God of Christianity, the God of Jesus, could be subject to any kind of change. For reasons which I will discuss in more depth in the next chapter, these Christians feel the need to defend the doctrine of impassibility, the teaching that defends God's unchanging nature and lack of passion.

In many ways and in many forms, Gnosticism infected other religions and philosophies. Christian thinkers such as the second-century Eastern father Irenaeus spilled much ink in opposition to its advance and influence. His magnum opus, *Against Heresies*, was a refutation of the wrongheaded thinking of many of these Gnostics. In it, he not only deconstructed Gnosticism, but also carefully constructed ways to talk about God's work in the act of incarnation.

What Irenaeus attempted was not something novel in light of the Gospels; rather, he restated the essential concepts:

- The incarnation revealed God's work to unite humanity with God.
- Jesus' redemption of humans involved the healing and wholeness of human nature, both in body and in spirit.
- Jesus' restoration of humanity through the act that Irenaeus terms recapitulation, in which Jesus *recapped* human history by living out his vocation, took place in the body and the story of Jesus.

What this meant for Irenaeus is that Jesus' story is *our* own story. Just as we live our lives in the flesh and in our own particular bodies, so Jesus lived his life in the flesh in his particular body.

An attack on the value of the body is an attack on this particularity of the Gospels, and an attack on the particularities of our own bodies and stories. This notion that God is here in this place, living in this time, in this specific manger or among those specific people, has often been expressed as the "scandal of particularity." Within the language of the incarnation, the concept of God as omnipresent, or everywhere, is no longer relevant. This is not to say that God, spoken about abstractly, may not be considered to be present everywhere simultaneously, but in terms of the person of Jesus, such talk is meaningless. If God is everywhere, then God is nowhere especially. Particular lives do matter, not to the exclusion of everyone else, but because of the value of those whose particular lives are threatened or who are in need. When we minimize the particularities of God's involvement within the drama of history, we minimize the impact Jesus has on our particular lives and stories. When we see the importance in God's here-ness, then we value the lives of others and our lives in this world.

THE BODY, DESCARTES, AND THE SCIENCES

Throughout the centuries, gnosticism crept into the crevices of the church, but it made some of its greatest advances as a result of the movement that academics call modernity. Modernity arose around the eighteenth century as a reaction to religious wars and was affected by technological innovation. At the time, the sciences, as established by Aristotle, were increasingly viewed as outdated, and questions about their premises became apparent. Philosopher René Descartes (1596–1650) attempted to question the reliability of the senses by tearing down the foundations of Aristotelian sciences.

It is important to note that philosophy and theology, which was known at one time as the "queen of the sciences," were never before undertaken in isolation. Plato's dramas were constructed as dialogues, Socrates's method was dialectic, and Aristotle wrote in reaction to his teacher Plato and to his contemporaries and predecessors. Augustine continued this trend in theology, writing some of his works as a conversation with an interlocutor or even with God, and the great medieval magister Thomas Aquinas (1225–1274) consistently interacted with philosophical and theological conversation partners of his day as well as with his predecessors. Similarly, much of Jesus' teachings were in response to or part of an interaction with another person, rabbi, or religious tradition. In the history of thought, there has always been an attempt at this kind of back and forth and relationship between conversation partners.

However, with Descartes, thought became a singular isolated "meditation."[9] Within this meditation, Descartes sought to begin with a single premise. He asked, If the senses can't be trusted, then what is the absolute bare minimum starting point for knowledge? Could he doubt even his own existence? Descartes came to consider skepticism as the starting place to prove one's existence. He reasoned that if one doubts that one exists, then the very existence of this doubt proves that one exists. Conversely, if one did not exist, one could not even begin to doubt. Therefore, doubt is proof enough that the doubter exists. Descartes summed up his conclusion in the famous adage "Je pence, donc je suis," or "I think, therefore I am."[10] This seemingly circular train of thought became a defining hallmark of Descartes's work and a touchstone for the modern world.

The greatest implications of Descartes's work were in the separation of each branch of knowledge from the others, and in the way we view the relationship between body and mind. What is the importance of the body? Are we our bodies? What may we do to the body? Who owns the body? All these questions and more were broken open by what is known as "Cartesian dualism." Descartes's thinking deeply influences how we in the West understand knowledge: Walk onto a college campus and you will see that the humanities building is separate from the science building. The study of business is conducted in one place, and the study of biology in another, with perhaps one course out of hundreds attempting an interdisciplinary approach. This is the Cartesian world.

But even more crucial than creating this epic divide is the fact that Descartes brought gnosticism back to Christianity. Because Christianity is always influenced by its cultural context, the Western view of Christianity was influenced by Descartes's dualistic view, which separates the mind from the body and the spiritual from the physical, and promotes the idea that we should look at the world in isolation rather than as part of and in dialogue with a community of knowledge.

What resulted from Descartes's influence was a shift in emphasis that has spread to many forms of Western Christianity, and includes:

- An emphasis on otherworldly existence (i.e., going to heaven), over God's present kingdom and this world

- An emphasis on theological ideas *about* Jesus (i.e., Christian doctrine), over the story of Jesus as found in the Gospels
- An emphasis on Christian belief, over and against Christian ethics (the study of the good and of how we practice it)
- An emphasis on spiritual blessings through material goods (i.e., the prosperity gospel), over the gospel of human flourishing
- An emphasis on spiritual salvation, over restorative and distributive justice, peace among peoples, and social concerns

Given that some forms of Western Christianity are more prone to Cartesian thought than others, I observe this duality playing out in many areas in the West and leading to many strange and conflicting ideas and values. Examples include a commitment to being "pro-life" but not pro-persons, and a belief in the "biblical Word" over the "living Word."

It is important to note that my argument here is not an anti-intellectual one that is *against* ideas. Ideas are important, but an emphasis on ideas over the concrete reality in which those ideas exist is a problem. The pursuit of ideas within the contained self, separate and autonomous, is at the core of my concerns. Christianity has never been simply a philosophy. It has always been concerned with a bodily existence—with how God exists *in a body*, and with how we exist in our bodies among the rest of God's creation, a relationship of both spiritual and material existence. At the same time, Christianity has never been an individualistic faith that is limited to the relationship between the individual and God; it has always been a religion of dialogue within a community that includes a multitude of voices.

Much of Christianity, and especially evangelical Christianity, has been given to this set of ideas:

- The inherent sinfulness and guilt of humanity
- The death of Jesus so that people can go to heaven (among some Reformed traditions, so that the elect can go to heaven)
- The importance of purity—religious, sexual, or otherwise

But these ideas are corruptions of the gospel, or at least the gospel outlined by Jesus and preached by Paul of Tarsus, and they contain no semblance of good news whatsoever. The story of Jesus is a story enfleshed in the human drama and in all things human. Jesus' story is not a simple story about the condemnation of God and salvation of sinners but is a story as complex as we are. God's involvement in human history was not solely to solve a problem, but it was and is a story of abandonment and love that is grounded in relationships with people and with the world in which we live.

Even though we are *not* entirely our bodies, our bodies are integral to who we are. I recall hearing an anecdote about a woman at her husband's funeral. The minister tried to console the woman by reassuring her that her husband was in a better place and that what they were lowering into the ground was not him, but an empty shell. The widow responded, "But that person being buried was the only one I knew."

Hebrew theology is thick with the perspective that we are enfleshed souls and soulish bodies. The second creation story tells of humans created from dirt and given animating life through the spirit, or breath, of God. The recorders of these Hebrew narratives had a difficult time speculating on existence after death because talking about life without a body was almost unimaginable for them. In the Old Testament there is no semblance of the Greek concept of an immortal soul.

Our bodies give us much of our knowledge of the external world. Descartes, however, did not trust that his senses, his body, were giving him a complete picture of the world around him. The people surrounding him might be androids, or "automatons," as he would say. But if the senses cannot be trusted and the outside world may be illusory, what is reliable? Descartes's philosophy depended on solipsism, the belief that only the self exists and that the self alone is the only person in the universe. It is easy to see the influence of this radical individualism in Western Christianity. Under Descartes's influence, faith is only between me and God, and is only about my salvation and what I can get out of my relationship with God.

One prime example of this is in the form of the Billy Graham "crusades." The goal of Graham's preaching was for people to make a confession of faith. Graham's ultimate concern was not for the common good of humanity or our relationships with each other and our world. Rather, the immediate need he sought to meet was individual salvation, the destiny of the soul. This was why his gospel dovetailed perfectly with Americanism.

In contrast, the early church had a much broader understanding of God's mission in the world. Individual salvation is of ultimate importance if one believes that the inevitable fate of humanity is damnation to hell, but this concern was not one of the early church. The Eastern fathers did believe in sin, bad choices, and incorrect ideas, but their goal was to tell a story of God's pursuit to free, restore, and unite humanity. In other words, they wanted salvation and restoration for the whole person, soul and body.

In the end, Descartes won the battle for our souls and minds. Reason devolved into individualistic bits of thought, truth became defined by the understanding that one spins for one's self, and there no longer was any way to bridge the divide between our minds and the real world. It is no surprise that we live in a time when even truth statements are questioned and the reliability of facts is challenged. Reality either seems too difficult to face or fails to bend into what we wish it to be. This is true not only of flat-earthers and creationists. Research has shown that we all experience confirmation bias, which leads us to place a higher value on observations and ideas that agree with our already established patterns of thought and what we already accept as truth, and to reject ideas and observations that are in opposition to them. If we face truth that conflicts with our understanding of reality, then we are challenged to change. We must admit that we do not have a monopoly on reality, and that to build our knowledge, we rely on something other than ourselves.

One way this dichotomy plays out is in the relationship that many evangelical Christians in the West have to science. People are often asked to choose between myth or science. However, this is asking people to make an unnecessary choice. Science is only a means to know, not knowledge itself, even though the word for science in Latin, *scientia*, means "knowledge." Science consists of experimental methods. It involves the testing of hypotheses, theoretical models, in order to prove them to be reliable. With repeated testing, science yields concrete results. Science has helped us find cures for diseases, created technologies that have made our lives easier, improved the ways we can connect to one another, and helps us live longer. Science brings us to conclusions that, in time, can come to be known as reliable facts. When "science" is shown to be inconclusive or is "disproven," what is disconfirmed is not science itself, but the available data and scientific technology and techniques.

Widespread skepticism about knowledge, scientific research, and irrefutable facts leads to grave consequences. For example, in the 1950s, it was known that smoking cigarettes was not safe. Much epidemiological evidence already existed that linked smoking to lung cancer and indicated that cigarettes were dangerous to public health.[11] This is counter to a commonly held belief that we did not know about the dangers of breathing smoke until much later. Philip Morris and other tobacco companies hired advertising firms to develop strategies to throw skepticism on this science, and instead created their own industry-based research firms, such as the Tobacco Industry Research Committee and the Council for Tobacco Research. These organizations attempted to produce disinformation about the causes of lung cancer among tobacco users.

Despite popular belief and current negative impressions, science emerged from the medieval period, known as the Dark Ages, when the church embraced the Aristotelian sciences, mediated by Islamic philosophy, which provided the basis for what have come to be known as the modern sciences.[12] However, one wrinkle in the timeline of progress stained the church's relationship with science. The controversy around the findings of Galileo Galilei (1564–1642) took place not during the medieval era, but during the Reformation period, and represented a political reaction rather than an act of religious inquisition. Galileo relied on the work of his medieval predecessors as a foundation for his science. The Italian scientist declared the heliocentric nature of the universe, with the sun at the center, to the objection of both the scientific and religious communities. Galileo was declared "vehemently suspect of heresy" by an inquisition in 1633. It was not until 1992 that Pope John Paul II admitted that the Catholic Church had committed errors in its prosecution of Galileo.

Today, the Roman Catholic Church does not hold such strong stances against scientific discovery but does oppose some of the ethical implications of science. Evolution is not as controversial in the Roman Catholic Church as it is in many fundamentalist and conservative Protestant denominations, because the Roman Catholic Church maintains a theology of immanence, the belief that God is present in creation and involved in the processes that make biological changes occur, rather than acting like a distant magician who causes changes in the created world to suddenly appear. In this regard, many Roman Catholic priests and theologians are consistent in taking a pro-life stance that includes opposition to abortion and the death penalty, as well as advocacy for the dignity of all humans, including the protection of immigrants. However, in some forms of Western Christianity, especially in the American South, science and evolution have become a political hot button. In the state of Texas, where I live, the "Scopes Monkey Trial" (regrettably so named because creationists opposed the idea that humans evolved from monkeys) is being retried in just about every educational board meeting where classroom curriculum is debated.

Certain segments of the church seek to again call into question the validity of the scientific method, even though they use the products that science provides. It is as if they believe that God created technology such as the cell phone but could not provide the basis for species to grow and evolve into the creatures they are today. The Cartesian axis separating mind and body has also caused a segment of the church to reject concerns about the environment and the way humans treat one another. Social and ecological matters are not separate from the Christian gospel (or from the teachings of the Jewish prophets), but a dualism of the mind holds otherwise.

It is possible to hope that people find salvation in Jesus but at the same time think and say and do all sorts of things against individuals and particular groups of people. We can recite John 3:16, "For God so loved the world," but simultaneously fail to love the world and fail to see that God gave God's Son to this world, not just to some people, but to the entire *cosmos* (Greek for world): the plants, the animals, the people, the universe. This division of mind eventually creeps into the rest of life, dividing it as well. Like our minds, our lives become divided and fractured, and as some parts of life are fed, others are left to atrophy. Some parts of life are valued and other parts are devalued. This division is deeply problematic when applied to people, and especially when applied to people who do not look, act, or think like us.

BLACK BODIES AND THE BODY OF CHRIST

- Terence Crutcher
- Philando Castile
- Samuel DuBose
- Sandra Bland
- Freddie Gray
- Walter L. Scott
- Akai Gurley
- Laquan McDonald
- Keith Lamont Scott
- Paul O'Neal
- Alton B. Sterling
- Christian Taylor
- Tamir Rice
- Michael Brown
- Eric Garner
- Stephon Clark
- Botham Jean
- Emantic Fitzgerald Bradford Jr.
- Jemel Roberson[13]

This list of African Americans killed in police-related encounters in the United States is nowhere near exhaustive, but serves as a
memorial for all those killed in such encounters, just as many gene-
alogical lists in the Bible represent the *taladoth*, or generations, of
God's people. Some early Christian readers who were ethnic Jews
were offended by New Testament genealogies because they included scandalous histories such as King David's adultery (Matthew
1:6). The names of these African Americans serve as a memorial
within the history of the United States, one that is rooted in the use,
fear, and killing of Black bodies. However, their names have been
in the headlines, for many too often quickly forgotten. Those whom

we memorialize are those whose lives we value. Although there is a memorial for the fifty-eight thousand American soldiers killed in the Vietnam War, there is no memorial for the more than two million Vietnamese lives taken because of the same war.[14] Do certain lives matter more than others? Why are some memorialized while others are not?

The clearest illustration of the way some bodies are valued over other bodies is in the violence perpetrated against them. In my home state of Texas, a deadly shooting took place in the home of an African American man named Botham Jean. Jean was a white-collar professional who was simply watching football in front of his television, like any other person on any given day in any given city in the United States, when a white police officer named Amber Guyger entered his residence and shot him to death. Officer Guyger claimed she mistook Jean's apartment for her own and, believing him to be an intruder, shot him twice. There are many questions that one could ask about this perplexing account, including how Guyger could possibly have mistaken Jean's apartment for her own when he lived one floor above her. To give Guyger the benefit of the doubt, she may have stepped out of the elevator too late or walked up one flight of stairs too many. But to enter a home and see an unarmed person eating ice cream and watching television, and respond by shooting him twice, is beyond comprehension and belief.

Let's reframe the situation another way. If Guyger had entered what she believed to be her apartment and saw a white woman watching football in front of the television, would she have shot? What if the person watching television was a white man? What if the person was a Black man in a business suit? What kind of racial "armor" would be required to prevent this shooting? Those who see a Black man and immediately regard him as a threat against their life are responding to an illusion of the mind, something that is not grounded in reality, but this myth is played out all too often. The

Black body is seen as a threat in a world that perceives some bodies to be inherently bad, and even evil.

Days before Christmas 2018, an eight-year-old boy named Felipe Alonzo-Gomez died in the custody of U.S. Border Patrol. Within the same month, seven-year-old Jakelin Caal Maquin also died in U.S. custody. During a social media discussion of this tragedy, one participant posted a picture of her own seven-year-old girl, commenting on how sad it is that our nation seeks to protect borders and not persons. I was struck by how painful and mind-boggling it is that many people would see the picture of this commenter's seven-year-old white child and not see the similarities to seven-year-old Caal Maquin. One child is brown and one is white. One is seen as less valuable and as requiring less protection, fewer resources, less love. It is a terrible irony that, especially during Advent and Christmas, a time when Christians await the arrival of God in the body of a Palestinian Jewish baby, some cannot welcome the arrival of other young people of color. Has Jesus become only an idea? Can Christians not see the baby Jesus in the persons of Alonzo-Gomez and Caal Maquin? Are Jesus' words, "Whoever welcomes one such child in my name welcomes me" (Matthew 18:5), not applicable to these children? Or are those words only for *our* children, in our own land, for documented children who are not brown, unlike the children to whom Jesus actually referred?

Christ is embodied both in the church and as a person. These sites of Christ's presence are tethered together as links that cannot be broken. But Christ's church is made up not only of those who profess to be Christians and attend church on Sundays, but also of "the least of these" (Matthew 25:45). They are the hungry and thirsty, the poor and sick, the incarcerated—that is, those in whom many of us least expect Christ to be present. They are the body of Christ as the church incarnate. As we treat these bodies, so we treat Christ. The story of Christ is not a story of people treating him well.

Jesus was a scourge on the political and religious systems of his day. He was seen as a heretic and rabble-rouser by the authorities and was tortured beyond what he could humanly withstand before he was put to death. It was in his physical body that Jesus was wounded and crucified.

Ignatius of Antioch (c. 35–c. 107 CE), one of the earliest apostolic fathers, declared of Christ's suffering, "For he suffered all these things for our sake, that we might be saved; and he truly suffered, just as he also truly raised himself."[15] Ignatius's intention was to strike down any doubt that Jesus appeared only as some kind of phantasm and did not suffer bodily. But it seems that Jesus is still seen as this kind of apparition by many Christians, who see him as someone who cannot suffer what we suffer, as someone who cannot feel pain and therefore does not intimately know our human pain. If Jesus is a person with whom we can empathize in his suffering, the same goes for those in whom Jesus is embodied, the poor and suffering. If we cannot believe in the bodily suffering of Jesus, we remain unable to see that the suffering of others is the same as ours.

Images of the suffering Christ or of those to whom Jesus came to minister, his fellow sufferers, are seldom seen in evangelical church buildings. Even more rare are images of the wounded body of Christ after the resurrection. The scars on Christ's hands, the wounds on his side, the bodily trauma of his suffering, is rarely depicted. In chapter 7, I will discuss how the wounds of Christ continue to exist, but for now I will simply say that in failing to depict the wounds of the resurrected Christ, the importance of the body is being erased, and the importance of the body of Christ in the world is being lost. Through our failure to depict bodily suffering, Jesus is becoming an idea, a phantasm, a mere notion, and not an embodied person. Historian Ellen M. Ross has shown how depictions of the battered and suffering Jesus in medieval England served as instruments of "curative sorrow."[16] This art helped viewers to respond to their own participation in sin, move toward acts of social and communal change, and receive healing for their own wounds. Because we rarely encounter such depictions of Jesus, our ability to see Jesus in the bodies of others, and especially in the bodies of "the least of these," is also being erased. Just as Nietzsche once declared that "God is dead," so we are declaring that "Jesus has left the building," at least this suffering, human Jesus.

The German pastor and theologian Dietrich Bonhoeffer saw the presence of Christ in the Black body. Bonhoeffer, during his 1930–31 year as a postdoctoral student at Union Theological Seminary in New York City, spent much time speaking to churches about post–World War I Germany. Bonhoeffer's theological upbringing was progressive, but also ingrained with the nationalistic tendencies that were deeply rooted in his culture. The method of much of Bonhoeffer's theological education occurred through the presentation of dialectics and the synthesis of opposing theological viewpoints, but Bonhoeffer could not reconcile the nationalism of Germany with the gospel preached by African American pastor Rev. Adam Clayton Powell Sr. at the Abyssinian Baptist Church in Harlem, where Bonhoeffer worshiped that year. Bonhoeffer scholar Reggie Williams comments, "Bonhoeffer's experience in Harlem demonstrates that a Christian interpretation of the way of Jesus must be connected to justice for a Christian to see beyond primary loyalties to self and kind, to recognize the needs for justice in another's context, and to 'love neighbor as self.'"[17]

While attending the Abyssinian Baptist Church, Bonhoeffer discovered the suffering God in the lives of Black Americans, an experience that later moved him to return to his native Germany, where he ministered to his people, spoke out against the Third Reich, and was imprisoned and executed for his resistance to the Nazi regime.

TRAVERSING THE DIVIDE

To truly understand another's perspective requires that we walk in their shoes, pour ourselves into their skins. Even if we share the same life experiences, true empathy is still a seemingly impossible task because every situation is different, and we cannot know exactly how another person feels. However, the attempt to see through someone's eyes through the act of being with them and standing with them moves us closer to knowledge, and this is what true divine love is about. It is situating ourselves next to another so they can reveal something to us, and we to them.

As a man, I am one of the least qualified persons to talk about the experience of giving birth. I do not know firsthand the bond between mother and baby in the womb, and I will never completely understand the experience of birthing a human being into the world, or of suffering pain in order to welcome life. Once while recording a podcast with two female cohosts, I asked a female author to read a poem that described her miscarriage. Both of my cohosts were deeply touched by the poem, almost to the point of speechlessness. My cohost Kate had herself experienced five miscarriages and was especially affected. I observed, heard, and could imagine her heartache, but I could only remotely understand her bodily experience, and knew that I needed to tread carefully on this hallowed and unfamiliar ground.

In discussing the possibility of God's suffering, the medieval theologian Anselm of Canterbury wrote that God knows our suffering, because God knows everything, but this knowledge of suffering is only purely intellectual. According to Anselm, God cannot know real suffering, because doing so would require God to experience change as a result of suffering, and in Anselm's understanding, God cannot change. For Anselm, a logician, God's claim, "I know your pain," is only theoretical and not real.

Does it make any difference in this world if God had real knowledge of human pain? Only the experience of living in the flesh allows one to give language to human experience. The Word did not know how to speak the words of human existence until it became embodied in this world. Not only were the molecules of life infused with God, but God became infused with the molecules of life. God's enfleshment involved both a crossing of boundaries and an allowance of boundaries to be crossed. Irenaeus points out that the way Jesus redeems our history is by being a part of every person's history at every stage of their lives, from birth to infancy to adulthood to death.[18] This is what Irenaeus called "recapitulation," or a retelling of history through the act of incarnation, or enfleshment. Jesus' story becomes the story of all humanity. His story is ours.

When the Eastern father Gregory of Nazianzus (c. 330–c. 389 CE) made the remarkable statement "What has not been assumed has not been healed,"[19] he was arguing that in order to heal every part of humanity, Jesus had to assume all of humanity in every possible way. For Gregory, the incarnation was the way that God assumed all of humanity and the way this healing took place. Because Jesus became human, aged, and experienced pain and even death, he could bring healing to all these aspects of human life.

Even though this is an important theological assessment of God's work of enfleshing human experience, a piece is still missing from Gregory's articulation of what God was attempting to do. While Jesus understood what it means to be a human, Jesus could not experience *all* of human existence. As a man, he could never know the human experience of childbirth, or of a menstrual cycle, or of other experiences that are particular to the bodily lives of women. And because he was a particular Palestinian Jewish man in the first century, Jesus did not know the experiences of Roman men or the particular experiences that I have had as an Asian American man living in the twenty-first century. Because of this, there remains a gap between our human experience and the fulfillment of God's absolute healing. Does God know *all* our suffering, pain, and joys? This is the relational chasm that we must face in relationship with a God who loves us. This relational tension is core to our experience of being human and living in flesh. In other words, it is within the space of moving near to us that God brings about the most love and the most healing. For example, as a teacher, I do not assume to know everything my students have experienced, even though I often tell them I was once where they are now. And so I attempt to know and understand; I attempt to see the world through their eyes in order to educate and guide them to be better persons.

As a human, Jesus could empathize with humans in a certain way that God could not otherwise empathize. Jesus' empathy came through his participation with humanity. Through the life of Jesus, God was no longer a spectator of creation, but became a part of creation. Jesus not only wades in the water, but immerses and bathes himself in the pool of our suffering and joys, hopes and dreams, disappointments and failures, in all of who we are and could be. Through the life of Jesus, God is in solidarity with the wounded and despised, with the heartbroken and oppressed.

For Jesus, bringing healing meant not only entering into a life of possible suffering, but also entering into suffering that he could not directly experience because of the physical limitations of life in his particular body. In identifying with humanity and becoming the representative of humanity, the Son of Man, Jesus took on suffering that he could not otherwise experience, especially that of the oppressed and suffering, by joining them in their lives. He inhabited the world of those who were demon-possessed, ostracized, and disabled, of those who were prostitutes or outcasts, or even just women. For God, entering human experience in Jesus meant entering the extremes of human experience, even "to the point of death—even death on the cross" (Philippians 2:8). But only in standing *with* and living *in* humanity was Jesus able to bring healing both to himself, by conquering death, and to others who had been broken by the world and its systems. In entering the extremes of human life, Jesus sees himself in them. Healing comes through Jesus' presence within these relational tensions: *being with, standing with, being in.*

The Scriptures, both the Hebrew Bible and the Christian New Testament, demonstrate the necessity of God's embodiment in order to relate to creation. The theophanies, the supernatural appearances of God, often occur in the form of angelic agency, in which angels not only represent God, but also embody God. In Hagar's encounter with the angel, she says "The LORD," naming the sacred name of God, YHWH (Genesis 16). This same angelic agency is seen in the LORD's appearance to Abraham (Genesis 18), in Jacob's experience of wrestling with God (Genesis 32), in Moses's encounter with the angel in the bush (Exodus 3), and in many other examples. And despite Hebrew theology that claims that no one could look directly at God, Moses is said to have known God "face to face, as one speaks to a friend" (Exodus 33:11).[20] These examples show God's initiative to move into human history, into our stories as an enfleshed person. God's intention has always been to be among God's creation, and not to remain removed from it. Jesus shows us the journey of this migratory God.[21] God's story is a story of joining us to make a dwelling among us, as the evangelist John writes (John 1:14). God's movement to set up residence among us as a stranger, a foreigner, occurs so that we are able to truly perceive God as God is and not as who we think God is or who we want God to be.

Crossing the divides created by the particularities of our embodied human experiences is difficult. I live in a city that is the most diverse in the nation, but is simultaneously one of the most divided. I am fortunate to live in a neighborhood in southwest Houston where my neighbors include people who are African American, African, Latinx, Asian, and white. I've had the good pleasure of eating with these neighbors, laughing with them, and even being despised by some of them. But my neighborhood is unlike many other parts of my city, where social and economic boundary lines are clearly marked, and crossing them in order to form authentic relationships is nearly impossible. What would be required for us to intentionally and positively transgress these lines and, in traversing this distance, to see God anew? How might we risk being *enfleshed beings*—entering into the world as God did, to be with the least of God's people? How could we move from the safety of our own places of comfort to the vulnerability of relationships with those whose lives are outside our spheres of comfort and safety? How might we enter into community with God in the fullest way, coming to know God's body as the body of the oppressed and marginalized, the body of those who are feared in this world? How might we bring healing to those lives, to those bodies, and in doing so, bring healing to our own lives and bodies? How will we join in the restoration of all creation?

Before we explore the ways in which Jesus binds up the wounds of those who have been harmed, it will be helpful to see the mission of God as a mission to enter into the life of the wounded and suffering. This will be the focus of chapter 3, which explores how God joins the world, not as a Roman citizen, a Pharisaic rabbi, or a temple high priest, but as the son of a lowly carpenter in a town from which no one expected anything good would come.

Recapitulation

A Greco-Roman rhetorical term meaning to sum up the main points of an argument (Greek ἀνακεφαλαίωσις; Latin *recirculatio*). In Latin, the term *caput* refers to the head or the chapter (of a book), so the idea of recapitulation is that Jesus summed up the life of Adam through his own life. Jesus is the "second Adam" who fulfilled a life of intimacy with God, whereas Adam rejected this kind of relationship with God and instead sought the power of the knowledge of the tree of good and evil. See Ephesians 1:10. Irenaeus of Lyons uses this term to talk about the redemption of humans by Jesus.

3

SINNERS, SIN, *HAN*, AND THE MISSION OF JESUS

I was naked and you gave me clothing, I was sick and you took care of me, I was in prison and you visited me.

—MATTHEW 25:36

He looks at his people and is deeply saddened that they are like wandering sheep with no one to guide them. Their lostness is not an absence from God—the divine has taken up residence next door. Rather, his people have become a diaspora—scattered seed, continually uprooted and replanted.

Their father Abraham and mother Sarah were also nomads and wanderers, foreigners and aliens.

Their ancestors were taken as captives to Babylon and then dispersed throughout the Near and Middle East.

Jesus and his people grow up under the oppression of foreign invaders. All he can remember is life in occupied lands and the governance of the Romans and the Herodians. Although the Herodian kings come from Edom and see themselves as Hebrews, they are aristocratic elites who rule with the same heavy-handed savagery as the Romans. His people are day laborers who tend land or work as stone masons and carpenters. The hands of his father, mother, and siblings are rough from work. Through the educational program provided in synagogues by the Pharisees, Jesus learns to read. Even at a young age, he can teach what he has observed—the kingdom taking root among us—and he slowly masters the art of storytelling. Working with his hands gives him the language and building blocks, not for revolution, but for restoration:

Day-laboring workers

Planting and sowing

Fig trees

Mustard seeds

Lending practices

Shepherding goats and sheep

Baking bread

Laying stone

Fishing nets and boats

As he teaches, Jesus code-switches between the vernacular of the masses and the subversive language of the kingdom, explaining to true disciples and students the meaning of all his metaphors.

His language weaves the fabric of an alternative reign. Stories form the cornerstone of his ministry and provide a framework for all the other things he does—the exorcisms, the healings, the miracles. But Jesus knows that he is still young and in formation. To heal the wounds caused by political structures and religious purists, he will have to find ways to dismantle those structures and to give new forms to what is honored and cherished in them—the Torah, the Law of Moses. These laws have been used to draw lines in the sand between the so-called sinners and those who see themselves as pure. But his people are prostitutes and outcasts, laborers and the oppressed. They are barely surviving, much less tending to hurts caused by others, and especially by those who are religious.

Some people take their destinies into their own hands. The Zealots are insurrectionists who pick up their swords to attempt a revolt against their oppressors. They are quickly caught, imprisoned, and crucified for their crimes. Other Jews of Jesus' day await their messiah, their anointed, who will lead a rebellion against Rome and restore the dynasty of David. Still others, the Essenes, give up hope in society and retreat into the Judean desert to live out their faith. They await the "Teacher of Righteousness" who will judge the wicked and bring his people into a messianic age. Jesus sees all these paths and possibilities, but he needs another way, a way that will not continue to inflict hurt on others, but that will confront and resist the political and religious powers. Jesus embodies both true forgiveness of enemies and a way to bring wholeness to his people, people with whom he sits daily, people with whom he eats and laughs and weeps, people whom he shows how to live in community. They are his people, and his rough hands will heal their hurts, mend their wounds, unbind their shackles.

THE GOSPEL OF THE *HAN*-RIDDEN

As a child in Vietnam, my mother learned French in a Catholic school, a remnant of colonization. Empire had brought religion with it. Christian colonizers looked upon the people of the world as "sinners" in need of saving. This is not too far from the perspective of the Roman Empire, which saw the rest of the world as barbarians in need of taming. With the colonization of a culture comes the colonization of language and ideas. The Christian history of the West is one of spreading the gospel of salvation for the sinners. Not only was this idea theological, but it also crept into the political and social structures of their empire.

For the early church, non-Christian pagans were not considered "sinners," but simply people who had not heard the message of liberation that would call them together for a better way and a better kingdom. But this message of liberation changed over time. Both Catholicism and the Protestant Christianity of Luther passed down the idea that humans are sinners who inherited the sin of their original ancestors, Adam and Eve, or who violated the law of God and were therefore condemned to eternal punishment in hell. Sinners need saving, and Christianity provided the salvation, presenting both the problem and the solution. From the cesspool of sin emerged the Savior of the sinners.

The term *sinner* was used as a religious code word for the "other"—those who were considered improper and impure, the "those people" of Jesus' day. The Pharisees and Sadducees used this term for those who did not or could not keep the Sabbath law by resting on Saturday. Sinners were considered to be religious law breakers, while the Pharisees lived lives truly separate from others, a lifestyle reflected in the origins of their name.[1] Jesus came to bring healing and wholeness to his people—to the "sinners." Jesus' people were those whom theologian Andrew Sung Park would describe as the *han*-ridden.

The term *han* has its origins in the Korean experience of repeated foreign invasions throughout the country's history. It is an almost untranslatable term, but means something like the feeling of having been deeply wounded, an inexpressible pain, a deep bitterness and resentment. The term *han* can be applied to those whom Jesus came to liberate and heal.

The philosopher Friedrich Nietzsche developed the concept of "slave morality," a view of morality that is born of being the recipient of extreme hostility. Slave morality is a response to oppression that is encapsulated by the French word *ressentiment*, or a feeling of deep hatred against one's enemies. Nietzsche used these terms to describe how the relationship between slaves and their enslavers creates a moral dichotomy in which the enslaved deem themselves to be "good" and their enslavers "evil."

Even though the term *han* is not used in the New Testament, it can be seen in the way in which the slur *sinner* was often used. Within Jesus' own culture, the term *sinner* was applied by the oppressors to those whom they saw as "other."[2] Their list of "sinners" was mainly made up by people who were laborers. Prostitutes were included because of their promiscuity, but so were shepherds, whose work kept them from observing the Sabbath, and butchers and leather tanners, whose work required them to deal in blood, making them ritually unclean. In maintaining a system of religious and cultural oppression, many of the religious leaders sowed *han* within the lives of those they called "sinners." In our own time and place, the analogous "sinners" are the people on whom many of us depend, but who are the outcasts in our society—farm workers, construction workers, restaurant cooks, the laborers who built much of the wealth in the West. The list would include Chinese railroad workers who made up 90 percent of the workforce of the Central Pacific Railroad Company but received less pay than their white counterparts. Among them would be those who were the target of the Chinese Exclusion Act of 1879, which Congress unsuccessfully sought to pass. They are the enslaved Africans whose whipped scarred backs provided the basis on which a nation was built. They are the brown refugees from south of our border who pick our crops, cook our food, build and clean our houses. They have become the subjects of policy debates in our time.

For Jesus, many of the religious people often functioned as a foil to demonstrate what false religion was like. Most did not comprehend the subtleties of Jesus' teachings, because of their narrow perspective on the Law, the Torah. Do not be like the Pharisees and Sadducees, Jesus said. "Whenever you pray, do not be like the hypocrites; for they love to stand and pray in the synagogues and at the street corners" (Matthew 6:5). The term *hypocrite* referred to the masked stage actors who appeared to be someone they were not. In a similar way, some religious people played the role of the righteous, but were dead and decaying inside, like whitewashed tombs full of filth (Matthew 23:27). There were scatterings of religious people, such as Nicodemus (John 3), who understood that Jesus was more than a peasant preacher, that he was a teacher with insight and wisdom far beyond his years. For the most part, though, religious people thought that they had already grasped God, and that others had failed to do so.

The problem with these religious people, teachers, and their followers was that analyzing the Law of Moses did not yield the righteousness they sought—righteousness not in bringing about justice for others, but in justifying their own deeds and existence. They discovered that in order to appear pure, others had to be considered less pure. Growing up in Nazareth, Jesus would have been educated in the Pharisaic tradition within a synagogue, where young men studied the Jewish religion and some prepared to become rabbis. Luke 4 narrates a story in which Jesus was invited to read a selection from Isaiah at his local synagogue, and then sit down and comment on what he had read. His audience would have seen this as quite an accomplishment for a "son of Joseph," a carpenter and day laborer. Jesus opened the scroll and read:

"The Spirit of the Lord is upon me,
    because he has anointed me

> to bring good news to the poor.
> He has sent me to proclaim release to the captives
>   and recovery of sight to the blind,
>   to let the oppressed go free,
> to proclaim the year of the Lord's favor." (Luke 4:18-19)

"Today this is fulfilled in your hearing," Jesus proclaimed. Jesus was claiming that liberation, healing, and forgiveness of debt were being realized right there in front of them. He was claiming that they were witnesses to a new era. Jubilee was finally upon them, and they would be unburdened and set free from Rome. But those present in the synagogue that day received Jesus' commentary as anything but joyous good news. Jesus proclaimed a liberation that was not restricted by nation or tribe to his own people, and he offered examples of non-Jewish foreigners who would receive the blessings of freedom and healing. This assertion so disturbed his audience that they sought to throw him off a cliff. Many in Israel believed that they were the chosen of God, and that everyone else, by default, was not. This was faulty reasoning on their part: while the first claim may well be true, it does not follow that the latter claim must be true as well. By excluding others, these pious people were also excluding themselves from Jubilee, from God's liberation and deliverance.

Jesus' program of freedom extended to and included those who were not the children of Israel. It also included all those who were part of Israel, but who were lowly and downtrodden, the poor and oppressed. The Magnificat, Mary's song of praise in response to the annunciation, is a song about such liberation:

> My soul magnifies the Lord,
>   and my spirit rejoices in God my Savior,
> for he has looked with favor on the lowliness of his servant.
>   Surely, from now on all generations will call me blessed;
> for the Mighty One has done great things for me,

and holy is his name.
His mercy is for those who fear him
    from generation to generation.
He has shown strength with his arm;
    he has scattered the proud in the thoughts of their hearts.
He has brought down the powerful from their thrones,
    and lifted up the lowly;
he has filled the hungry with good things,
    and sent the rich away empty.
He has helped his servant Israel,
    in remembrance of his mercy,
according to the promise he made to our ancestors,
    to Abraham and to his descendants forever. (Luke 1:46-55)

Mary was most likely a teenage girl; she was viewed as chattel, without citizenship or legal rights. The lowly social status of women during Jesus' time is illustrated by one of the prayers used by Jewish men each day, which included the line "Praise be God that he has not created me a woman."[3] Mary's song is an amazing hymn of defiance in the face of such oppression. There is no subtlety or political correctness in it. She boldly declares, "God has filled the hungry with all things good. God has pushed out the rich people, leaving them empty-handed."

There is no way to "spiritualize" Mary's message or lessen the blow of her condemnation of the rich and powerful. Those who hear her sermon must either absorb it as the shape of reality or avoid it altogether. This vision that Mary proclaimed was growing inside her. She was going to give birth to this upside-down kingdom that she nourished in her womb. The pain of bringing forth this new reality would be not only the pain of childbirth, but the pain of all that Mary experienced in her life. Her life was full of hardship, including the delivery of a child near an animal manger, carrying a child during the forced migration from Bethlehem to

Egypt to escape the infanticide perpetrated by Herod the Great, and many other social and economic hardships that resulted from living as a Jewish woman in Roman-occupied territory. As Mary's own hardships and woundedness came to a creative juncture with God's own willingness to dive deeply into the waters of suffering, her wounds birthed the source of healing for the world.

Jesus' statement that the Son of Man (*ben adam*) "came to seek out and to save the lost" (Luke 19:10) contains this aspect of healing and protection. Jesus' mission was not to rescue people from the fires of hell and eternal punishment—no one who has become lost wants to be lost or deserves to be labeled a "sinner" as a result. Rather, those who are lost are like sheep who have wandered from the fold and need protection from the perils of predators.

SINNERS AND THE SINNED-AGAINST

In the book *The Sinner*, the German writer Petra Hammesfahr presents the story of a mysterious murder that occurs without any apparent motive. The main character, a woman named Cora, murders a seemingly random man during an otherwise normal visit to a lake. Hammesfahr slowly reveals that both Cora and her disabled sister were subject to religious and physical abuse in their home as they grew up, and that their overly religious mother has applied the label "sinner" to them. Cora commits a sin by murdering the nonthreatening stranger, but the story presses readers to question which character is the real sinner, and how the sin of abuse might be manifested in other acts of sin.

The early Eastern fathers did not believe that people were born "sinners." They did believe that there is an "originality" to sin, in that there was a moment when sin first took place, but they did not conclude that Adam and Eve's disobedience in the garden of Eden led all people to inherit their sin. The doctrine of inherited sin was developed by Augustine, the fourth-century bishop of Hippo, who promoted a view of sin in which all people are judged guilty at birth because they have inherited the sin of Adam. Augustine saw inherited original sin as specific to Adam because it was Adam's "seed" that passed the sin down to his children.[4] Augustine, who read the New Testament in the Latin translation rather than in the original Greek, interpreted the Latin version of "in Adam all have sinned" to mean that Adam's sin was the *cause* of humanity's sin.[5]

This interpretation resulted from Augustine's misinterpretation of a passage in the letter to the Romans (5:12). A standard translation of that text from the Greek would read:

> Therefore, just as sin came into the world through one man, and death came through sin, and so death spread to all *by which* all have sinned.

In Jerome's Latin translation, used by Augustine, the same verse reads:

> Therefore, just as sin came into the world through one man, and death came through sin, and so death spread to all *in whom* all have sinned.

The difference between the translations is not substantial, but a surgeon's scalpel is not needed to dissect it. The first translation portrays death as spreading to all humanity *because* of Adam's sin. This death is infectious, becoming characteristic of the world in which we live. We often react to this death with sin. Death is the problem that we and God must confront because death has become the source of sin in our lives.

In contrast, the Latin translation of this verse indicates that sin *causes* death to spread through all humanity. In Adam's sin, we "all have sinned." The infection of sin passes from Adam, "in whom" all have sinned, to us, exempting no one. We are all born into sin and are immediately guilty as sinners. To expunge our sins, we need to be baptized; the younger our age at baptism, the better. Infant baptism literally became a way to cleanse the guilt inherited from Adam.

The Eastern fathers who could read the original Greek New Testament understood Romans differently and did not see it as teaching the doctrine of original sin. They held that rather than inheriting sin, humans inherited shame, and that the consequence of death was a reminder of the mortality all humans face because of Adam's disobedience. They insisted that no one should be punished for the sins of their parents, but only for their own sin.

To understand how shame can affect a family system, consider, for example, the convicted criminal Bernie Madoff, who was sentenced to 150 years in prison for cheating thousands of investors of $65 billion in the largest Ponzi scheme in history. He was found guilty and will serve a federal prison sentence for the remainder of his life. His two sons maintained their innocence and did not participate in any way. But Mark Madoff, Bernie's oldest son, committed suicide, presumably because of the shame he faced as a result of his father's actions. During his trial, Bernie Madoff admitted, "I have left a legacy of shame."[6] This is a more plausible explanation of how shame leads to continued hurt than Augustine's explanation of inherited guilt and sin.

Eastern church fathers believed that all humans suffer shame for their inability to have the kind of relationship with God that they were meant to have, the kind enjoyed by the representative first couple in the plentitude of the garden. This shame was evident in Adam's attempt to hide his nakedness when God asked, "Where are you?" (Genesis 3:9). Rather than experiencing fellowship and intimacy with God, each other, and the earth, we—like Cain, the son of Adam and Eve—wander the earth without a home or identity. It is this longing and searching that are the hallmarks of humanity.

THE CONFLICT BETWEEN AUGUSTINE AND PELAGIUS

At the council of Carthage in 418 CE, Augustine argued for his theology of inherited guilt. His opponent was Pelagius, a Christian theologian and ascetic. Augustine disputed Pelagius's teachings about free will and original sin. Pelagius had written a letter to an aristocratic follower, Anicia Juliana, who was seeking moral council for her fourteen-year-old daughter, Demetrias. Pelagius's response to her included a case for human moral responsibility:

> We accuse God of a twofold lack of knowledge, so that he appears not to know what he has done, and not to know what he has commanded; as if, forgetful of the human frailty of which he is himself the author, he has imposed on man commands which he cannot bear. And, at the same time, oh horror! We ascribe iniquity to the righteous and cruelty to the holy, while complaining, first, that he has commanded something impossible, secondly, that man is to be damned by him for doing things which he was unable to avoid, so that God—and this is something which even to suspect is sacrilege—seems to have sought not so much our salvation as our punishment![7]

Pelagius outlines a scenario in which God gives people laws that cannot be obeyed. This indeed sounds like the God that Augustine described. However, Pelagius argues that if this is the case, then we are accusing God of two counts of ignorance: That God has forgotten about human frailty in requiring humans to do what humans cannot do, and that God has condemned humans to be punished for what they could not do in the first place.

Pelagius's argument can be illustrated with this example: Imagine that I'm a father to a two-year-old child, someone I've created (albeit not on my own). I impose a rule for the house: all people living under my roof must take out the trash on Thursday in order to earn their keep. My two-year-old does not take out the trash on Thursday, so I tell her that she must leave my house. This is her punishment for violating my law.

Augustine's stream of Christianity seems to describe a relationship with God that is similar to this. Augustine argues that God has given the law, which humans violated, and therefore they must be punished. In challenging this doctrine, Pelagius raised serious questions about human responsibility and free will. Pelagius's ethical point is that *humans are only responsible for actions over which we have free will.*[8] If we cannot obey a law with complete intention, then we are not responsible for obeying it. My two-year-old cannot be responsible for taking out the trash, because she is simply not capable of doing it. Laws must be made in such a way that people are able to keep them, and any system of government based on the reverse is unjust.

Take another example: God, through Moses, gave the Decalogue to the Hebrew people in the wilderness because their minds were conformed to the laws and practices of living in Egypt. When Moses reported God's self-declaration, "I am the LORD your God, who brought you out of the land of Egypt, out of the house of slavery; you shall have no other gods before me" (Exodus 20:2-3), was Moses saying, "God is asking you to fulfill these commands, even though God knows you cannot do it, and God is going to punish you for failing to do it anyway"? Of course not. The Egyptians had made statues to their gods, so that was what the Hebrews understood. As a result, when YHWH led them out of Egypt, they made a golden calf to worship YHWH. God gave them the law to transform the mindset that enslaved them to certain thoughts and notions of

God or the gods. These laws were not set up with the intention of causing them to fail. It is humans who make God out to be a cruel rule maker, law enforcer, and judge, not God. God's intention was not and cannot be a no-win scenario.

Augustine argued for "original sin," the understanding that the guilt of Adam and Eve was passed on to all humanity through sexual reproduction. Adam passed on his sin through his seed, making the body both the retainer and channel of evil. This doctrine of inherited guilt was not shared by Augustine's Eastern counterparts. Jesus did not preach it (and at times he preached the contrary), nor can it be found explicitly in the Scriptures. In fact, one scriptural counterexample appears in Ezekiel 18:20: "The person who sins shall die. A child shall not suffer for the iniquity of a parent, nor a parent suffer for the iniquity of a child; the righteousness of the righteous shall be his own, and the wickedness of the wicked shall be his own."

It seems blatantly unjust for a person to be condemned for the sins of someone else. If I commit a crime, should my children be convicted even if they did not participate in the crime? Unless we define justice in an arbitrary way, there is no universe in which such a conviction would be considered just. Even so, Augustine was adamant about countering the Pelagian heresy and sought to excommunicate Pelagius from the church. Augustine saw Pelagius's doctrine as nullifying Christ's work of salvation. If people could honor the law, Augustine reasoned, then what would be the purpose of Christ's death? His argument rests on the assumption that the sole purpose of Christ's death was to appease God's wrath about human violation of the law. (We will explore this point further in chapter 4.)

Augustine was attempting to submit his elaborate theory of original sin to the church by refuting Pelagius's doctrine. This was Augustine's version of a theological "legislative rider"; he hoped his doctrine of original sin would be approved by attaching it to a separate theological argument. The victims in this theological dispute were Pelagius and his followers.

Around 416, Augustine and four other bishops wrote a letter to Pope Innocent I advocating that Pelagius and Celestius, a teacher and follower of Pelagius, be excommunicated until they recanted their views. After the death of Pope Innocent I in 417, Pelagius wrote a letter to the succeeding pope, Zosimus, demonstrating his reliance on the orthodoxy of the church. Celestius convinced Zosimus to reopen the case and thereby not condemn Pelagius. But with the help of Emperor Honorius of the West (395–423), Augustine and other African bishops were able to mount another attack against Pelagius and his views. At the council of Carthage in 418, theological heavy-handedness and political expediency won the day, and Pelagius was excommunicated. Theology, like history, is written by the victors. The Eastern bishops present at this ecumenical council did not speak out against Augustine's view of original sin. It remains, to this day, part of the dogma of the Roman Catholic Church.[9]

Pelagius and his followers believed in baptism and that sin originated with Adam, but they did not believe baptism was necessary for salvation. In their view, humans became enslaved to sin and Satan because they had been deceived by the "evil one." Jesus gave his life as a ransom (Latin *redemptio*) in order to liberate us, luring the evil one to take his life rather than the lives of humanity. In the resurrection, God raised Jesus from the dead, in effect tricking the evil one. The deceiver was deceived, and freedom was provided for all. In this view, the purpose of Jesus' life was not merely transactional; it was also transformative. Jesus' death and resurrection provided a way to restore human nature and return humanity to proper relationship with God.

In the end, Pelagius was banished from Jerusalem and allowed to settle in Egypt with the permission of Cyril, patriarch of Alexandria. His teaching ministry may have continued, but his work after the date of his exile is lost to us. Pelagius was the casualty of political expediency, and his name a byword for *heretic*, even though his work is invaluable to the history of theology.[10] Pelagius wished to raise the bar of ethical standards, moving the church away from "cheap grace," to use Bonhoeffer's term, but instead he became a whipping boy for Augustine's view of free will and original sin and a straw man for those who rejected grace and exalted humanism. Only history could give Pelagius a fair trial, but in fifteen hundred years it has not yet done so, and the Reformation only strengthened Augustine's case.

RANSOM IMAGERY OF THE EAST

In the history of Christian theology, the Eastern church's view of redemption work is known as the "ransom" theory.[11] This theory emphasizes the liberation of the deceived from the evil that bound them. Ransom theory depicts God as fighting the forces of evil in the world.[12] The Eastern fathers believed that systemic evil and sin, which can be understood literally, psychologically, and spiritually, cause the enslavement of people.

We experience slavery of all kinds that the early Eastern fathers address in different ways. The history of slavery in Europe and the Americas demonstrates how oppression exploits human beings by turning them into tools of production. Many forms of mental slavery, including addictions that run rampant, especially in wealthy nations, can take us captive. They trap the spirit and mind, and even though they are not "sin" in themselves, they result from brokenness, abuse, and mistreatment. Often, those who become addicted are self-medicating to cope with other issues, such as traumatic experiences.

According to the Eastern fathers, evil persists in the world spiritually and infects our structures of life, community, and government. When I say "spiritual," I am talking about the core or essence of a person or structure. When evil infects an organization, it takes over the core values and ideals of that organization, a phenomenon that we can see in governmental corruption and abuses of power. When Paul talks about the struggle that is "not against enemies of blood and flesh" but against "spiritual forces" (Ephesians 6:12), he is not talking about spirituality in some vague and general way, but is speaking about the Roman Empire that likely arrested and imprisoned him in Rome during the time he was writing this letter. Paul advocates against taking up arms to oppose the government, calling Christians instead to take up a "spiritual" armor and sword (Ephesians 6:10-17).[13] Often, the problem we face is not evil people, but systems that are given to evils that manifest in violence, hatred, and the condemnation of others. These systems enable people to perform evil deeds and perpetuate evil, and both perpetrators and the oppressed need liberation from them.

What the Eastern fathers demonstrated in their interpretation of God's work in the world was holistically restorative. They saw God as a healer of the sin-sick. God freed humans by restoring and bringing them into unity with God. As Irenaeus of Lyons and Athanasius of Alexandria argue, God became incarnate so we might become more godlike. Greek Christians called this process of becoming more godlike "divine restoration," or *theosis*. Theosis is more than a makeover; it is an upgrade to our humanity that involves both restoration and evolution. God sought not only to heal humanity in mind and body, but to make mind and body like God, and to reunite humans with God, restoring our original purpose as created image bearers:

Then God said, "Let us make a human in our image, according to our likeness." . . .

So God created the human in God's image,
    in the image of God, God created them;
    male and female God created them.
    (Genesis 1:26a, 27, translation mine)[14]

In Hebrew, as well as in the Greek translation, "image" and "likeness" are different words, and they held different meanings for the Eastern fathers.[15] To be made in God's image is part of all human existence; we all are created in God's image. However, we come to reflect God's likeness through the work of the Spirit of God and through imitation of Jesus' life and of the lives of those who have lived in God's likeness. The Christian journey involves moving away from the forces of evil and toward a life in the divine likeness of God. Just as two people who know each other for a long time come to resemble each other, complete each other's sentences, and know what makes each other tick, so as one comes closer to God, one becomes more like God.

One aspect of liberation that the Eastern fathers did not emphasize in their theory of redemption is the struggle between the sinned-against and sinners. How did sin enter the picture, if not through the sin committed against those who are victims of sin? Contrary to Augustine's view of inherited sin, it is not possible to be a sinner just in general. There is always an object to my sin. If I am a liar, then I must be lying to someone. If I am a thief, I must be stealing from someone. When I lash out in anger, however justified, this sin is committed against something or someone. Within the act of sin, there is always a sinner and always a person who has been sinned against.

Historically, theologians like Anselm of Canterbury and John Calvin have treated God as the primary person against whom we sin. But Minjung theology, including the work of Andrew Sung Park, shifts the focus of the offense from God to humans, or even to the earth and other animals.[16] However, in the story of Western Christianity, we seldom see the two differentiated. Within the theory of inherited sin, we have lumped together those who have committed sin with those harmed by that sin, declaring everyone to be equally sinners.

Many have applied the apostle Paul's writing to the Roman church as a defense of the view of the inherent sin of all: "All have sinned and fall short of the glory of God" (Romans 3:23). But when Paul wrote this letter to this particular group of Christians, or group of house churches, he meant to call out his Jewish counterparts for their belief that they were the chosen and righteous and that others were not. This was a rhetorical strategy to help him gain support from Jewish Christians to reach out to Gentiles; it was not meant as a thorough analysis of the problem of sin.[17]

For Jesus, the term *sinners* was a misnomer, a label used by religious people to differentiate those who upheld the Jewish laws from those who did not. Jesus was often criticized for eating with "sinners" and tax collectors. Consider the story from Mark 2, in which Jesus heals a paralyzed man by saying, "Your sins are forgiven." Jesus' words do not indicate that he believes the man's sins caused his paralysis (as evidenced by Jesus' words in John 9), but are a way to demonstrate "that the Son of Man has authority on earth to forgive sins" (Mark 2:10). In response, the scribes, the Jewish legal experts, question "in their hearts" who had the authority to forgive sins. Jesus confronts them, asking, "Which is easier, to say to the paralytic, 'Your sins are forgiven,' or to say, 'Stand up and take your mat and walk'?" (v. 9). Jesus' point was not to indicate that this man deserved the label of "sinner," but to show the religious people that so-called sinners were not in a permanent state of sin and that sin is neither inherent to their being nor incurable. They simply need healing, and this was, for Jesus, "easier" than forgiving sin.

Later, Mark depicts a scene in which Jesus sees the tax collector Levi at a tax booth and calls him to be a follower. In response, Levi invites Jesus to dine at his home, and of course Levi's tax collector friends show up. These characters in the story are called "tax collectors" and "sinners" intentionally by the gospel writer. If *sinner* were just a general term to be applied to all humanity, the different designations would be meaningless. But Mark is careful to differentiate these categories in the text, indicating that we need to read them as important to the way he tells the story.

The "scribes of the Pharisees," the legal experts of the legal experts, observe this and make a point to talk about it. They see that Jesus is hanging out with the "unclean" of society. Tax collectors were viewed as traitorous scum who took in money for the Roman government and skimmed some off the top for themselves. The Pharisees and others in Israel turned up their noses at them and wondered why any Hebrew, much less a Jewish teacher, would want to associate with them. However, Jesus responds to the scribes in this backhanded way: "Those who are well have no need of a physician, but those who are sick; I have come to call not the righteous but sinners" (Mark 2:17). Jesus was *not* saying, "You religious people are well, you don't need healing, you are perfect." (They perhaps needed healing most of all.) Jesus was speaking truth, tongue in cheek.

The sick, says Jesus, are those oppressed by the law and standards of the religious leaders. They are the sinned-against. The *real* sinners are the religious leaders, and God's healing is extended to those whom the religious people have hurt and labeled as "sinners." The scribes, Pharisees, and Sadducees created a dichotomy between those who were good and those who were bad, the holy and the unclean. This duality continues today in Christianity. The "sinners" are those who do not believe in and conform to certain moral codes, while the holy people are those in the church. In Roman Catholic terms, the holy are those "in communion," and the unholy are those "out of communion" with the church.

I attended a Roman Catholic university for five years of my graduate education, learned the Hail Mary in Latin, and even attended Catholic mass several times. After one service, I commented to a Catholic sister about the beautiful service, adding that I could not, of course, take communion, because I was at that time a Baptist. This sister replied that I was unable to take communion because I was "out of communion" with the church. I sincerely asked, "Who is in communion with the church?" "Those who say they are," she replied. "So it is only in name," I asked, "that we can distinguish who is in communion with the church and who is out?" "Yes," she admitted. This is a regrettable turn of logic that pronounces one group "in" and another group "out," simply by confession. The "sinners" are like the Dalit caste of India, those seen as the lowliest. Even though the least of Israel were not born into their status, they might as well have been.

Jesus was interested more in the so-called sinners than in the religious people because it was his mission to bring healing to them, to liberate them from the oppression of those who would impose this burden on them. The religious people were the real sinners, but their veneer of righteousness prevented them from seeing who they really were and that they were the ones who really needed salvation.

When I was first introduced to Christianity at the age of eighteen, I was taught that sin was merely a violation of God's law, that God was keeping tabs on the things I did, both as law enforcer and judge, and that some of my actions were transgressions against God. (This is also when I first learned about Protestant "purity laws"— rules about sex, drinking, cussing, smoking.) Both the Hebrew and Greek words for sin, *chatá* and *hamartia,* respectively, mean "to miss the mark," but interpreting those terms without context gives the impression that God wants all our actions to be perfectly direct-ed toward some arbitrary goal. If we don't accomplish that perfec-tion, then we are sinners! I was declared to be a sinner and told that I needed salvation from my sins, but there was so much more to the story than I was led to believe.

I later came to realize that sin takes on both the weight of action and of intent within the relationships around us. In other words, sin is something that causes us to be out of harmony with the world, out of harmony with the real intent for which we were created. This disharmony is how some of us "miss the mark." It might be helpful here to introduce a definition of sin that is grounded in what actu-ally takes place in relationships. This definition is both specific and broad, so as to encompass arenas of life to which many people do not realize an understanding of sin can be applied: Sin is a violation of the law of love towards God, humans, and the earth. When we fail to love the Creator of the universe, the universe, and everything in the universe, we have failed in what we were born and created to do. We fall short of the intended purpose for which we were made. All life, purpose, and meaning flow from the movement toward love; sin is a corruption of this internal drive.

For much of Western Christianity, the one sinned against has been understood to be God. Anselm of Canterbury writes, "To sin is nothing other than not to give God what is owed to him." And, Anselm asks, what is God entitled to? Complete righteousness. Failing to give God this perfection dishonors God.[18] Sin has robbed God of God's honor. John Calvin says something similar: "Original sin is seen to be a hereditary depravity and corruption of our nature diffused into all parts of the soul, that first makes us liable to God's wrath."[19] He concludes that we have inherited a condition about which God is angry.

Were Anselm and Calvin not aware that God is not the only victim of sin? People sin against other people, as well as against animals, the environment, the earth. When we deforest land without thought of the environmental impact, when we pollute streams without thinking about who will drink the water, we are sinning against *both* others and the land. Genesis ties Adam and Eve's disobedience to the earth (Genesis 3:17-19).[20] Seeing sin as segregated to one area or another is a failure to see creation in its entirety. It is another symptom of our broken mentality, and a sin in itself to separate our lives into these disparate components. Jesus sought to integrate the various aspects of our brokenness so healing would be holistic rather than affecting only an isolated part of us. To be healed, we must see that some woundedness is caused by others, either as individuals or as part of a system.

This division between sinner and sinned-against is not academic, but entirely practical. If a person sees a doctor because of a headache, the doctor will not simply say, "Take two aspirin and call me in the morning." The physician will analyze the source of the symptom. The headache might be caused by an environmental trigger or by something internal. It could be caused by brain cancer, or it could be just a relatively mild occurrence. But the treatment must reflect the cause. Western Christianity has not approached the problem of sin in this way. The problem of sin has been dealt with not specifically, but only generally, and therefore sin persists in the form of all sorts of evils in the world. The "sinners" are blamed for the source of sins, and the problem repeats itself in an ongoing cycle.

Scapegoats litter religious history, reflecting the problems caused by failing to delineate sinners from the sinned-against. Christian theologians seem either to argue that "those people are sinners" or, when Christians have committed heinous acts against others, to invoke the blanket statement that "we are all sinners." This approach is not only unhelpful, but also perpetuates other acts of sin in the world.[21] Until a larger recognition of this difference occurs, we will continue to hear the rhetoric of "we are all sinners" as a way to gloss over the problem of the relationship between the sinner and the one sinned against.

A CULTURE OF *HAN*

As noted, the word *han* describes the deep woundedness of the Korean people. *Han* is a sense of unresolved victimization that can lead to anger, hatred, and violence. The history of Korea is a history of *han*. This small country has been the focus of attempted conquests from the Japanese and Chinese and has faced multiple conflicts with the United States.[22] *Han* is a ubiquitous theme among the people of Korea and lies just below the surface of Korean culture. Related terms exist in the Vietnamese language: *hận* (hatred) and *oán hận* (animus or ill-feeling toward another because of an offense).[23] It is no surprise that the Vietnamese borrowed this term from the Korean language, given that Vietnam has a similar history with China, Japan, France, and the United States.

In the United States, "the blues," which originated in African American culture, is the equivalent term for *han*. The blues are ingrained in music and lyricism in art. Where cultures and people are oppressed, a concept similar to *han* exists in their language and grammar. Korean American theologian Andrew Sung Park refers to the killing of Abel, and the spilling of his blood, which cries out for justice, as an image of *han*.[24] In this story of sibling rivalry, Cain kills his brother and seemingly suffers no consequence. Abel's blood, which has saturated the ground, cries out on his behalf for justice. *Han* is the groaning of the victim whose wounds are unvindicated, without redress. But what happens when *han* remains untreated? When the victims of *han* are not healed, a cycle of *han* may develop, leading to continued violence not only toward the perpetrators, but also toward additional innocent victims.

Consider this example: A little girl suffers abuse. She is an innocent victim. No one would label her a "sinner" or blame her for causing the abuse. But victims of abuse need treatment. What happens if she does not receive treatment for the trauma caused by her abuse? What happens if violence then begets violence, and the cycle continues? Unless the *han* is treated and the wounds healed, the cycle will only repeat.

The deep wounds of the United States have been largely ignored. As a consequence, we continue to bleed out, both physically and in our psyches, repeating the cycle of hurt, blame, and denial. The history of European expansion and colonization is a history of sowing *han* into the land. Wounds, including the taking of Native lands, forced resettlement of First Peoples, mistreatment of Chinese laborers, enslavement of Africans, segregation of African Americans, internment of Japanese Americans, mass incarceration of African Americans and other people of color, and many more systemic wrongs continue to scar the landscape of the United States. Thus far, political attempts to heal this history have not brought resolution.

In 2009, Senator Barack Obama became the forty-fourth president of the United States. Obama, who was born in Hawaii to an Irish American mother and a Kenyan father, was seen as a hopeful leader who could heal America's past. But despite all of President Obama's progressive reforms, the United States did not find healing under his leadership, and during the years after Obama's presidency, deep divides that had been festering beneath American life came to the surface. In a 2018 speech, Obama said that the present political state of affairs is only the "symptom" and "not the cause." The real cause, he argued, is "rooted in our past, but it's also born out of the enormous upheavals that have taken place in" our lifetimes.[25] We remain a "house divided," perhaps even more so than before. The wounds of our history lead us to keep waging war on each other, and many of our political responses do not seem to heal the problem, and instead exacerbate it.

In the years during and after Obama's presidency, white supremacist groups have become emboldened, and there has been
an alarming increase in the rate of unjustified shootings of African
Americans and people of color. The Federal Bureau of Investigation
reports that for three consecutive years, 2015 through 2017, the
number of hate crimes grew. Between 2016 and 2017 alone, the
number of hate crimes motivated by race or ethnicity increased by
18 percent.[26]

African Americans, who have historically been the target of
slavery, torture, lynching, and all forms of hatred and violence,
continue to be targets of fear and violence. The dominant narrative
many historians and people have told has not been about the dangers posed by white enslavers, angry cross-burning Klansmen, or
white soldiers crossing into foreign soil wielding muskets or M16s.
Instead, Black and brown bodies have been portrayed as a threat to
peace and security, leading them to become targets of hatred and
scapegoating. These injustices were not absent during the Obama
years, and they have not been dealt with holistically and thoroughly. The "hope" of the senator's campaign slogan turned into a mis-
placed optimism that did not treat the sickness still remaining in
this country. Symptoms point to causes, and these causes are not
cured with a change of policy or change of administration, but only
by facing the roots of our past and problems.

The healing of *han* is challenging because there is no quick or
easy fix. Simply saying that Jesus will heal the *han* of the world
will not accomplish that healing. Neither the Gospels nor any
New Testament writings attest to this. The Gospels do show *how*
the wounds of the world are healed, and give witness to the hope
that comes from living in cooperation with God's kingdom, creating a healing community. In speaking of a healing community, I
am speaking of something larger than the church or any particular denomination. Churches, parachurch groups, and other groups

can be part of this kind of ministry, but in order for the deep divides in our culture to be resolved, we cannot remain in separate groups and ideologies. We need thoughtful programs of reconciliation and healing that move us beyond diversity training and cultural awareness, although those initiatives are still needed as well. The historical trauma of the United States needs to be handled with the same intensity and delicacy as were post-apartheid and post-Rwandan genocide reconciliation and justice strategies. Given the stories we tell about each other, these strategies must address the ways in which we are perceived and how we relate to each other.

The scope of this book is limited to the ways that the ideas of our religious past have contributed to our present situation. This is only one component of the problem, but it is a very important one because it undergirds our culture in the United States. Religion is ingrained in our culture. The word *culture* has two sources. One comes from the idea of cultivating (Latin *colere*); that is, we sow ideas, values, attitudes, norms, and behaviors into our society and expect a result. We create a culture in order to "form a more perfect union." The other meaning comes from the Latin word for religion, *cultus.* All cultures are like religions, with languages, rites, rituals, practices, and beliefs specific to each culture.

In the United States, we have a culture based loosely on "Judeo-Christian" values, which permeate every part of private and public life.[27] This framework undergirds many of the systems in which we all participate. By nature, this culture has racial and economic overtones, because in order to allow some people to advance and achieve the "American dream," others must remain at a disadvantage. This culture is also intimately connected to the religious values and beliefs of many Americans. Religious dogmas and doctrines have supported this culture of injustice, and because they are such an integral part of our lives, like the air we breathe, we don't easily see them.

The religious beliefs that undergird cultures are sometimes easier to see in a culture other than our own. Some African cultures believe the myth that people who are albino have healing properties and hunt them to use their bodies to cure certain diseases. Those albino Africans who survive this brutality may be missing appendages. Most of us in the West find such practices appalling and backward. However, we have our own myths that play out in our society and that are equally violent and primitive. Many of us continue to perpetuate these ideas because we are unable to take a step back to see that they are a problem.

For example, in many Christian groups, a pervasive concept is what theologian Walter Wink terms "the myth of redemptive violence," the notion that God uses violent methods to solve problems, and that the violence is therefore justified. This myth supports attitudes, policies, and behaviors in our country. I am *not* suggesting that the solution is *only* religious, but this aspect is one that has seldom been analyzed and is an essential part of addressing root problems.

In response to cultural myths such as the myth of redemptive violence, Christianity either is seen as the problem, causing people to abandon it, as has happened in many European countries, or is transformed into something different. When people leave Christianity, the result is an increase in secular myths and values that eventually harm rather than help. For example, Denmark is currently struggling to accept those of different cultures and religions, although they are a "progressive" society that contributes much to the social good of their people.[28] Their secular values have evolved into a form of cultural conformity, a type of fascism, that has left their culture unable to embrace diversity. Secularism has become a new form of religion, with its own language, rituals, and symbols.

JOINING THE WORK OF THE KINGDOM

This is a crucial time for Christians to reenvision the kingdom in terms of the mission of Jesus in the world: to heal the *han*-ridden; to liberate people from bondage to their wounds and from a system of wounding and woundedness; to actualize the forgiveness of debt, both monetary and psychological; and to proclaim good news to those in poverty. This is a vision that provides meaning and purpose for those stripped of their created intention. If we do not become co-creators in this new endeavor, we will continue to face tide after tide of destruction in the form of resentment, anger, and violence.

To paraphrase Jesus' proclamation in Luke 4, "The time has come. The kingdom is at hand. Rethink and believe in the good news."[29] The news of the kingdom must be good news to those who need it, and may be bad news for those who resist the message that this world will be toppled. The first Christians experienced the kingdom as encroaching on the dominion of the present world. Demons were cast out, people were healed, and lives were changed through those whom Jesus empowered to join in establishing God's new realm and reality. But the forces that Jesus resisted were the same forces that arrested, tortured, and executed him. Jesus was tried as a traitor to his own country and became a death row prisoner.

———

I was born in Quy Nhơn. Between this coastal town and Pleiku is an area known as Mang Yang Pass, where in 1954, Communist Vietnamese troops retaliated for the years of French occupation by attacking and killing six hundred retreating French soldiers. They were buried there standing up, facing France. These French soldiers were part of a task force called Groupement Mobile 100 and some of whom were veterans of the Korean War.[30] This ambush resulted in the last battle of the First Indochina War, known as the Battle of An Khê. The attack on them was as much a symbolic act as it was one of aggression. I would like to think that the wounds of war die with each death of a Vietnamese or American veteran. But wounds are not only in the body, but also in the psyche, and not only of individuals, but also of the collective. They continue to live and breathe—resurrected by inability or unwillingness to resolve the conflicts of the past and therefore to make peace when new conflicts arise.

Will we turn around and look at our past, make space for grief, closure, and healing? Or will we continue to let our wounds fester by denying our hurt and continuing the cycle of creating victims and producing perpetrators? The memory of history does not die but lives on in us. We inherit the racism and conflict of the U.S. Civil War and all wars past. Do we intend to send our daughters and sons to fight these same wars in their futures because we ourselves have not made peace with our pasts?

Han

한

The word *han* is an almost untranslatable word used to describe the deep woundedness of the Korean people. *Han* is a sense of unresolved victimization that can lead to anger, hatred, and violence. Han is a loanword from Chinese (恨) and is related to the Vietnamese words *hận* and *oán hận*, translated as "hatred" and "animus," respectively.

4

GOD AGAINST THE MACHINE

The principle cause of suffering for the leper is not an annoying, smelly, itchy skin disease but rather having to live outside the camp. So the call is to stand with them, so that the margins get erased and they are welcomed back inside. Jesus doesn't think twice: he touches the lepers before he gets around to healing them.

—GREGORY BOYLE, *Barking to the Choir*

He suffers the push and pull of being human. As crowds gather and his reputation increases, he seeks to be alone. He retreats into prayer and meditation, within the quiet of his soul, to find rest from the demands placed on him, to refill what was poured out. His strength is not isolated and individual but comes through his dependent connection with divine Parent and Spirit. It is in this relationship that he finds renewal and makes connections with others and the universe. As he breathes deeply, he prays. His prayer is each breath. The air filling his lungs, *ruach*, spirit. With each inhale, he receives; with each exhale, he lets go. This is how he heals people and performs miracles and teaches—in connection and through inner connection. It is in this breathing and listening, this mindfulness and emotion, that he operates.

At the synagogue, the place of religious education, a man tormented by an unclean spirit recognizes this "Holy One of God." Here, in this most unusual of places, the "unclean" and the "holy" meet. Where else could this man, plagued by demons, go? Jesus has had similar encounters in the desert and is not unfamiliar with the language and appearance of demons. He silences the spirits, and they depart as quickly as the man had appeared in the synagogue.

At the invitation of Simon, one of his disciples, Jesus enters his home and sees Simon's mother-in-law, feverish and bedridden. She had no access to the advanced healthcare that we have today, not even to the painkillers that so many of us take for granted. Jesus lifts her up, lowers her temperature, and brings restoration to her body.

Throughout Galilee, Jesus tours the towns and brings the message of the kingdom. Moving seamlessly between exorcisms, healing, and teaching, he sees his work to be for those afflicted and neglected. He weaves a web that ties the world together, a world torn apart by abuse, apathy, greed; by unjust actions. He seeks to mend rather than to break apart, to sew rather than to shatter.

But the momentum of the world in which he lives works in counterstep to this kind of life, persistently breaking connections rather than making them. A system exists that seeks to gain power through violence and wealth. It is not about unity but about divisions and discontinuity—in this sense it is demonic. It preys on the weak and vulnerable, the lowly and despised. The religious leaders and Judean kings, the Roman governors and imperial soldiers: all live off those who are indebted to them, which gives them power. The many exist to provide for the few. In contrast, Jesus' mission is to serve the many. He insists to his disciples that this is the way of the new world, the coming kingdom. But this new reality is difficult for them to swallow because they have been enslaved to this system for their entire lives. They are like the Hebrews who left the slave pits of Egypt and, when asked to trust in the provision of YHWH God, had to be discipled in order to follow and learn. They try his infinite patience, and as they learn, he learns. An all-knowing grasp of the universe is no longer available to him. He seeks to love, and love means the risky business of giving up and being open to what people offer him, open to the point of death. He will need to reflect on this more each day, this bothersome and troubling mortality.

THE POLITICS OF JESUS

The graphic novel *Watchmen* depicts an alternative reality that takes place during the Cold War, with Nixon serving as a fifth-term president and the United States emerging victorious from the Vietnam War with the help of an omnipotent godlike superhero named Dr. Manhattan. Dr. Manhattan teams up with the most intelligent man on earth to produce an energy source that will end all world conflict. They reason that since wars stem from a lack of resources, eliminating the scarcity of energy will eliminate the need for war. But in our own universe, wars are fought not only over resources, but also over ideas and power. War determines who controls these resources and therefore who owns the power.

The United States, of course, lost the Vietnam War, or as it was called by the Vietnamese, the American War. The war began because of conflict between the ideologies of communism and democracy. After World War I, in 1919, Hô Chí Minh, the father of the Communist revolution in Vietnam, attempted to gain support from the United States in his quest to gain independence from France. He and a group of Vietnamese nationalists drafted a letter to President Woodrow Wilson, writing under the pseudonym Nguyễn Ái Quốc

(Nguyễn the Patriot). Minh expected that the United States would be sympathetic to the Vietnamese, since the United States had struggled for its own independence from the British. However, Minh's attempt was ill-fated. His letter, handed to the U.S. Secretary of State at the Versailles peace talks, was never passed on to Wilson. Minh turned instead to the Soviet Union and China for support of what would later become the Communist revolution in Vietnam.

World War II formally ended on September 2, 1945, when, aboard the battleship *USS Missouri*, Japan surrendered to the Allies, agreeing to an armistice signed by French general Philippe Lelerc. On the same day, Hồ Chí Minh, drawing on the words of the American Declaration of Independence, declared Vietnam's independence from France: "We hold the truth that all men are created equal, that they are endowed by their Creator with certain unalienable rights, among them life, liberty and the pursuit of happiness."

But these words did not compel the United States to aid Hồ Chí Minh or the Việt Minh forces that would rise up to defeat the French. The ensuing Anti-French Resistance War eventually resulted in a unified Vietnam under a specific brand of communism.

Governmental systems and societal structures are not built overnight. Their ideas and ideologies are rooted in a complex array of policies and strategies, of programs and institutions. The structures that built the trade in enslaved people in the West originated in Enlightenment thought, which was also key in constructing the modern world. Views of the relationship between the government and the individual, the nature of property, and human rights all emerged from ground-shifting events such as the French Revolution of 1789. This was inspired in part by the American Revolution, which birthed the complex history of race in the United States. The movements that sought to bring peace to the wars of Europe and America also brought colonization and slavery. It was no coincidence that the industrial age was also the age that saw certain peoples as tools and instruments for profit. Governmental structures in general, and politics in particular, all deal with the governing of what they deem to be scarce resources. Government is concerned with determining who gets what and how they get it. Jesus' struggle was against a political system and a related religious system that sought to make these determinations.

The words *political* and *politics* come from the root word *polis*, or city. Politics concerns life together as a people, how this life should happen, and what form it should take. When Jesus talked about the kingdom and kinship, he was being political. This was a direct affront to the empire of Rome and the political leaders of Israel. When writers of the New Testament refer to the "messiah" or "Christ," they are intentionally invoking the title of "anointed one," usually reserved for the kings of Israel. Neither Jesus nor his followers were ever apolitical or nonpolitical. Until Constantine, they were understood to be revolutionaries, offering an alternative to the politics of Rome. The ministry of Jesus continually opposed both a system of scarcity and a view of personhood that defines some as less than divine image bearers, a view resulting from a perspective of scarcity. Both of these aspects of Jesus' ministry are political in nature.

Scarcity and the image of God are at the core of how politics operates in both Jesus' world and ours. Scarcity has to do with how we view our resources and the distribution of those resources. The image of God has to do with how we view people, either as image bearers of the divine or as something inferior, as objects and instruments for our use. For Jesus and his followers, the kingdom of God confronted the scarcity problem involved in most political structures by manifesting a system of abundance. The God who created "the heavens and the earth," the entire cosmos, continually provides God's creation with sustenance. Jesus was a homeless, penniless itinerant preacher who consistently depended on the hospitality of others for provision. In calling his disciples, he saw how some of his people left the stability of their own careers to follow him. Within the context of seeming insecurity and struggle, Jesus assured them that God was providing for their every need (Matthew 6:25-34). His miracles of feeding the crowds attest to the continual creative acts of God.[1]

The notion that God creates and continues to create is a notion found in the early church and in the work of Thomas Aquinas in the late medieval period.[2] Usually creation is viewed as a past act, something that God did several billion years ago. The notion that God once created, and then left creation alone, is a modern and deistic view of God that portrays God as a watchmaker who winds up the clock and leaves it alone. The continually creative God is involved in a unique work that is described as more than just "making," and involves artistically bringing forth new life. God is not just a designer or engineer, but one who gives birth. There is an intimacy between the created work and God.

Many times, I have built tables in my workshop. Creativity is involved in this work even before I hone pieces of wood and nail them together, which is just construction. Creativity involves both imagination and the physicality of the materials. It also involves a personal relationship between the creator and the created. My tables are not products of an IKEA manufacturing plant. They are personal pieces that were made specifically for someone or a particular purpose and context. Similarly, God's creative work is one that continually takes place in the lives of people in order to free them, to liberate them from the system of scarcity that tempts them to reach for seemingly better fruit.

Related to the problem of scarcity is the view that all people are co-equal image bearers of God. It is no coincidence that political systems govern how humans are perceived: as citizens, subjects, property, aliens, prisoners, or refugees. All these designations have a legal status given by governments. In a feudal system, peasants are not of the same status as landed gentry, and therefore are not given the same rights, protection, and resources. Similarly, in the United States, enslaved Africans were seen as property without the rights of citizens. Not until the Snyder Act of 1924 were all Native Americans given equal citizenship, even though the Fifteenth Amendment, passed in 1870, stated that all U.S.-born people receive the rights of citizenship regardless of race. And it was not until 1920 that, with the ratification of the Nineteenth Amendment, women were given the right to vote—and even then this was largely extended only to white women. The Voting Rights Act of 1965 extended these rights to African Americans and all other citizens regardless of race. All these views of citizenship and voting rights point to how governments view individuals.

Minjung theology seeks to address the needs of the oppressed, from whom the political system has taken power, by focusing on the need to heal *han*. This way of thinking and talking about God goes back to the 1970s when a group of theologians and lay leaders were dismissed from their seminaries and university posts for criticizing the South Korean government. The notion of Minjung draws from the oppressive history of the Yi Dynasty (1392–1910), when those who were excluded from the elite and ruling class were called the Minjung, or the "masses of people." This longest-lived imperial reign in Korea planted *han* deeply within the people of Korea. During the Japanese Occupation (1910–1945), those who were not Japanese collaborators were oppressed, taking on the status of the Minjung. Andrew Sung Park describes Minjung as "those people who have suffered from exploitation, poverty, socio-political oppression, and cultural repression throughout the ages. They know the pain of dehumanization."[3]

The political system determines who is considered fully human and who is not. In other words, "humans" are treated with dignity and respect, are given rights, and have inherent worth. Christians are called to see all humans as divine image bearers—a profound realization if one understands that bearing "the image of god" refers to the status of emperors and kings in the Near and Middle Eastern context. Being created in the image of God is not solely a spiritual concept. The image of God is the complete person, body and soul, the entire human, and not only a person's mind. The image of God is enfleshed in humanity, and all bear this mark, but this understanding has not been shared throughout Christian history. As Christianity joined with the power of governments, those who were image bearers and those who were not became carefully differentiated because, if power was a scarce resource, it could not be granted to everyone!

SCARCITY IN A NATION OF PROSPERITY

My family came to the United States as refugees fleeing a war-torn nation. My father was an officer in the South Vietnamese Army, and going to the States was a move for survival, rather than for opportunity. In Vietnam, we were middle-class, in the top economic strata by Vietnamese standards. Both of my parents had well-paying careers, as was evidenced by the nanny that my parents employed to watch my brother and me. We left a life of relative wealth with only what fit in our suitcases. For other families leaving Vietnam, especially for those who became known as "the boat people," this was not the case. They saw the United States not only as a place of survival, but as a land of dreams. This is perhaps how the United States is seen by many immigrants—as a land of hopes and dreams. But this land, seen as abundant and plentiful by some, is perceived by many others as a land of scarcity.

Perhaps the First Peoples who lived in this land and knew no strict boundaries or did not believe in the idea of real estate saw this land as one of abundance. But for many who colonized this land, the Americas were not seen in this way. In their view, there was not enough to go around, so land and resources were taken rather than shared. Like selfish children, they divided up the land and forced people out of their homes and into less desirable habitats.

Old Testament scholar Walter Brueggemann identifies Pharaoh and Egypt as biblical images of scarcity.[4] Egypt, for the Hebrews, was not only a place of physical slavery in service of the building projects of Pharaoh, but also a place of bondage to the mentality of not having enough. In the biblical narrative, Pharaoh is in constant fear that there are too many Hebrews. He seeks to eliminate the Hebrew males because he sees them as direct competition for power.

The narrative of the Old Testament is one of scarcity and abundance. The Hebrews came to the land of Egypt to escape a famine that ravaged the land (Genesis 47:13-27). Joseph, a Hebrew who lived as an Egyptian, helped his family escape the famine. But years passed, and while the Hebrews stayed in Egypt, there were changes in power. A new pharaoh arose who "did not know Joseph" (Exodus 1:8), and the Hebrew people became seen as a threat to the Egyptian people. The Hebrews were enslaved into forced labor and their first-born males killed. For Pharaoh, there was not enough to go around—not enough power, not enough wealth, not enough food, not enough land. Some people would be the "haves," and others, the many, would be the "have nots." The have nots were forced to sacrifice on behalf of the haves, trading the lives of the few for the many. But God sent Moses, who grew up in Pharaoh's court, to liberate the Hebrews from their bondage.

Moses was the epitome of a person with a mentality of scarcity. He grew up with power and privilege but did not yet understand how to use them. "Who am I that I should be sent?" (Exodus 3:11) he repeatedly asked YHWH God. Even though he was born a Hebrew, he had been adopted by Pharaoh's daughter and, until he realized that his own people were being mistreated, lived within the confines of the court. Repeatedly, YHWH God told Moses that

God would be at Moses's side to perform miracles through him, but Moses did not see how he could speak. His reluctance was not a matter of eloquence, but of authority. Moses possessed authority but did not know how to use it. Pharaoh's court had taught him to see lack rather than plenty. Pharaoh could not understand how he could liberate a people who were his private property. Moses's insistence, "Let my people go," was met with further hardships placed on the Hebrews: they were forced to make bricks without straw (Exodus 5), the equivalent of saying, "Build a house without wood!"

After freeing the Hebrews from captivity, YHWH God taught the Hebrew people how to depend on God's abundance through daily provision. Even though they were physically free, their minds were still in bondage, and in the wilderness the people complained. They claimed that they would rather work in the slave pits of Egypt than worry each day about sustenance. But God provided food from the sky in the form of mysterious quail and manna.[5] They were instructed not to save up the food. Instead, they were told to depend on God to provide it fresh each day. We see a similar teaching in Jesus' prayer of provision, "Give us this day our daily bread." It is a prayer for abundance, asking God to provide each day all that we need. When they needed water, the Hebrews complained, and God provided water from a rock (Exodus 17:1-5). This became the back-and-forth tension between YHWH and the Hebrews: they "grumbled" against God, Moses took their complaint to God, and God provided for them. The complaints were born from a mentality of scarcity that they learned in Egypt. Wandering in the wilderness for forty years was a way to unlearn this way of life before the Hebrews entered the land of "milk and honey."

The irony of life in the United States is that we are in a land with plentiful resources, but because of fear, greed, and the mentality of scarcity, we are depleting these resources to the point that one day neither we nor future generations will have them. Once the American buffalo, or bison, roamed the land by the millions, but they quickly became nearly extinct because of unsustainable ranching practices and an attempt to starve Native peoples. The enslavement of Africans for cheap labor was another form of scarcity. Slavery involves viewing people as nonhuman and valuing profit above human dignity. Lack of immigration reform, especially for people of color, speaks of how many citizens of the United States do not understand their own histories of immigration. I once asked a group of Christians a simple question, which many could not or did not want to answer: "How is it that Christians believe in a God who is the creator of everything and provider of everything, and at the same time some can think that other people are coming into this country to take things away from them? How is it that we believe that we *own* or possess this earth?"

People either trust Pharaoh or trust YHWH God, worship either mammon or God. Perhaps many Christians truly do believe in a pie-shaped world and are still living with an Egypt-like mentality. Many Christians believe that the resources on this earth are limited and need to be cut up and portioned out. They believe that if another person gets a piece, then they cannot get a piece, or that they'll need to get a big piece first to prevent everyone else from getting one. But these Christians are not living in circumstances analogous to those of the Hebrews in Egypt; their life circumstances are more like those of Pharaoh, who sought to enslave people because of his perspective of scarcity. These images of scarcity contrast with the images of provision in the kingdom of God, with Jesus' exorcisms and miracles, and with the open table of the Last Supper. Jesus, who was born in the midst of an infanticide aimed at taking his life, sought to tear down this system of scarcity.

In August 2017, Hurricane Harvey hit the Gulf Coast as a Category 4 storm, leaving many neighborhoods in Houston under water. We had just been visited with the Tax Day Flood (April 2016) and the Memorial Day Flood (May 2016). In Meyerland, a neighborhood close to mine, I met a homeowner who'd had to rebuild all three times. During Harvey, about fifteen thousand homes in Houston were devastated, and the cost to rebuild was nearly $200 billion. Neighborhoods and houses near the bayou were underwater, but our house, at sixty-five feet elevation, stayed dry. I did not stock up on many supplies before the storm, because we had a pantry and two freezers full of food. Two guests were staying at our house, and we managed to feed them for a week, providing three square meals a day. We are not rich, but middle-class, and had more than enough to go around.

When the rain stopped and I was able to leave my neighborhood, friends put me on lists to lead groups doing demolition work, since I had some contracting experience. I loaded up my wife's SUV with my tools, and headed to the first homes closest to me, in Meyerland. This is a predominantly upper-middle-class and upper-class neighborhood, and the houses had been submerged in water up to five feet deep. Remnants of the water line marked each house. I noticed a common theme—people were holding on to their sewage-soaked "valuables" like hoarders on a reality television show. They had a difficult time piling their belongings onto the mountains of debris and furniture that were slowly lining the sidewalks and front yards and spilling into the streets. They had difficulty letting go of what was now an accumulation of garbage. I can understand grief over the loss of possessions and the trauma of living through a disaster. But in a land where possessions are kept in air-conditioned storage facilities that provide better living conditions than many people have in other parts of the world, these people acted as though they would never be able to replace their possessions. The disaster was tough on them, but their behavior also reflected the reality that we have built a world where many have come to believe that the replaceable is irreplaceable, and vice versa.

Jesus' world was one of abundance. It was not one of wealth or prosperity, but of fulfillment and flourishing. Not extravagant, but enough, and even more than enough. His kingdom consisted of showing the abundant nature of God's being, that there was more than enough to go around, that we can *both* have and share. Jesus offered an option other than hoarding or indulging extravagantly, the alternative of living fully. Jesus often said, "I have come so that you can have life and have it to the full" (John 10:10, translation mine). These words have been spiritualized to mean something like "I have come so you can go to heaven." But "eternal life" is about quality of life, not quantity. Eternal life is about living in the liberating fullness of God.

Another image of abundance can be seen in theologian Diana Butler Bass's use of the word *table* for the kingdom.[6] For Jesus, the meal is where God reveals God's abundance. "This bread is my body, broken for you; This blood is my life. Poured out for you."[7] God sustains the world through God's body. This table is not for a few or only some, but for all who will sit and partake. Despite denominational doctrines that claim otherwise, no one has a monopoly on true communion with God. It is an act of vulnerability on God's part. It is an open-armed invitation extended to all who would "taste and see that the LORD is good" (Psalm 34:8). However, meeting at the table is vulnerable not only for God, but also for us.

Sitting at the table with all people often means we will sit with those we do not like or care to know. We will sit at the table with perceived enemies or those foreign to us. We may be invited to dine with someone of a different ethnicity, cultural background, skin color, political affiliation, sexual orientation, or belief system. Living in the kingdom is a scary prospect, especially for those who have lived under the system of Pharaoh. To eat with each other reveals our deepest vulnerabilities: that we share the same hunger and thirst, that we are not exempt from needing others.

In the East, Middle East, and Near East, hospitality is part of the cultural DNA. To welcome strangers into your home, to give them food and drink, to share your possessions with them, is both a way of "killing the enemy with kindness" and a way of outdoing your neighbors with good deeds. In the biblical narratives, welcoming the stranger is often a way to welcome the divine (Genesis 18:1-15; 1 Timothy 5:10; Romans 12:13). Hospitality codes were ubiquitous in the East, despite a seeming lack of resources. In Vietnamese culture, it is said that if one has a guest, one finds the guest extremely precious and will slaughter the last of one's animals in order to prepare a meal for the guest.

Even though there is a culture of "Southern hospitality," especially in small Texas towns, the general culture in the United States has grown to be, at best, marked by suspicion and fear of the stranger. Current restrictions on foreign travel, the xenophobic attitudes toward those who are not white (both noncitizens and citizens), the increase in restrictions on immigration, and the detainment and separation of children from families (even of those who are seeking amnesty as a legal means of migration) are all motivated by an attitude of scarcity. These practices also speak to the intrinsic "worth" of some people and the devaluing of others. If all people are "children of God" and all land is created by and belongs to God, how can some people be more worthy or less worthy to live in a particular place than others?

In his judgment discourse about the separation of sheep and goats, Jesus claims that God is found in those whom we least expect (Matthew 25:31-46). Neither the "sheep" nor the "goats" recognize Jesus in the incarcerated, the sick, the naked, or the thirsty. But the sheep still provide presence and provision for them, while the goats do not. God is present to them not through *knowing*, but through the *act* of seeing those in need as someone like us. How can the white soccer mom in the suburban United States see that the incarcerated Black man is like her? What is the divide that must be bridged in order to welcome the stranger into our own homes, places of business, and spheres of influence?

SEEING THE IMAGE OF GOD IN EACH OTHER

Race is a social construct that was created to conquer and control others by separating them. At the root of the racial problem is the problem of scarcity. Racialization is economic, a way of placing an economic value on differences. Take, for instance, the history of Chinese workers in United States. A large part of the labor that produced the first railroads was done by Chinese immigrants. The Central Pacific Railroad employed over twelve thousand Chinese workers in the 1860s, but soon afterward, the Chinese Exclusion Act of 1882 forbade these same workers, who had become legal residents, from becoming U.S. citizens. Fear of Chinese people was termed the "Yellow Peril," a way of painting Chinese people as a primitive and subhuman species that did not deserve any rights. The term *yellow* was used to set Asians apart from Black people and other groups, even though people of Asian descent, like me, often have skin tones found in both white and non-white people. In entertainment media, the character of Fu Manchu was created as an Asian caricature to reinforce the idea that Asians are always scheming and evil (ironically, this character was often played by an actor in "yellowface"). This was a strategy to further set one "race" apart from the others in order to prevent the sharing of the economic and social wealth of this country.

My friend Rev. Phoebe Niranaza-Wabara, who survived the Rwandan genocide, tells of the stories created to separate Tutsi and Hutu tribes. European colonists, mainly from Belgium, gave Rwandans these ethnic designations in order to form rivalries between groups of Rwandans and therefore control the Rwandan people. The colonists differentiated Rwandans into one of three distinct races: Tutsi, Hutu, or Twa, and propagated the myth that Rwandans were indeed three separate peoples, even though Hutus and Tutsi often intermingled. The resulting divisions led to rivalry, suspicion, and struggle for power among these groups, and eventually resulted in the Hutus gaining the majority power, which culminated in the Rwandan genocide of the mid-1990s. Hutus saw the Tutsi as "other" and, as a result, engaged in mass slaughter of men, women and children. Between half a million and one million people died as a result of this war.

The history of colonization and white supremacy is a history of scarcity. The trade in enslaved people in the West dehumanized people and saw them only as tools in a larger economic machine. "All men [people] are created equal" was only applicable to those considered a person, and did not apply to those who were no longer deemed human. In the United States, slavery provided cheap labor and increased profits for white enslavers. After the Civil War, the segregation of Black people and Jim Crow laws created continuing forms of economic exclusion.

These patterns of economic exclusion have shaped the allocation of property and wealth in America, where, as in many countries, land is a way to retain wealth and ensure that one's family can inherit property and resources, often with appreciated value. Property ownership enables many Americans to buy homes and invest in their retirement and provide for their children. But what if one is prevented from purchasing property? Until 1968, the U.S. Federal Housing Administration (FHA) prevented many African Americans from purchasing homes. The FHA would not provide financial backing to home builders who constructed houses for African Americans and made it illegal to sell FHA-backed homes to them. Houses were built exclusively for white people in order to create whites-only neighborhoods. In addition, the FHA did not lend money to African Americans seeking to purchase homes. Through unfair lending and sales practices, called "redlining," Black people were prevented from accessing wealth in the United States.

Lastly, the inequities of the U.S. justice system, which has resulted in the mass incarceration of African Americans, has prevented many African Americans from sharing in the economic wealth of America.[8] While African Americans comprise only 12.3 percent of the population, and while white people and people of color commit crimes at the same rate, African Americans make up a disproportionally large percentage of those within the prison system. We have a criminal justice system that disproportionately puts Black and brown people in prison. It is not blind to skin color—in fact, the system is built on fearing people with certain skin colors over and against others.

The system that is designed to lock up people of color is also designed to make a profit for others. The incarceration system, which is a billion-dollar-a-year industry, was privatized in order to move incarceration out of the public sphere and into an arena where corporations can make a profit from incarceration. In such circumstances, justice is not, and cannot be, blind.

Some critics see this form of racism simply as a form of tribalization and claim that similar discrimination occurs in all cultures. However, white supremacy, the notion that "white" or "whiteness" is more valuable than other people groups, is a specific form of discrimination that is prominent, systemic, and structural, and is not universal. White supremacy has created the racial constructs, boundaries, and disparities within American society. To simply call white supremacy tribalism is to revert to the idea that "all people are sinners," as discussed in chapter 3. Because our culture is shaped by the social construct we call race, we cannot be "colorblind." Doing so is a way to avoid being confronted by how we treat others, privileging one race over another. As noted earlier, Jim

Wallis calls racism the "original sin" of America. We cannot forget this part of our cultural identity, and the more we can accept it, the more we can deal with it.[9] However, if we deny its existence, we will return to the same hurts and wounds in an attempt to deal with the past in ways that are not constructive.

Let me illustrate this problem with a story that I often see replayed in my own life and in the lives of many people. Children often do not want to see themselves as reflecting the character of their parents. This is especially true if they perceive their parents to be mean or abusive, which can make it very difficult for children to accept the reality that they are like their parents, in both good and bad ways. My father is a very kind and generous man, but he has a very quick temper that is easily ignited because of either a real or perceived wrong. I see both of these aspects in myself and in how I relate to others; I can be very kind and generous, but when a Houston driver cuts me off, watch out!

This flash of anger is something that needs to be controlled. For many people, it is very difficult to see and accept this reality about themselves, and many children attempt to form their character in ways that are completely different from that of their caretakers. This is both an attempt to see themselves as different and a way to guard from having to work on personality traits that they believe are unacceptable. It is easier to criticize and hate others than it is to see the flaws in ourselves, as Jesus warns when he speaks about removing the two-by-four from our eyes before trying to remove the splinter in the eye of another (Matthew 7:3-5). But this is often not a healthy way to live; it is reactive rather than reflective. People who cannot exist courageously in their own skin often have trouble in relationships, and may move from one to another. They often see this as the fault of others and not themselves, because they cannot see themselves in others, especially in those whom they dislike. They are bitter and resentful toward parental figures, but find friendships and romantic relationships with people who are similar to their parents, and often repeat the same relational mistakes.

This is the history of the United States. The history of violence and hatred is so horrendous and so painful that many Americans cannot see themselves in it. Often, when people use the term *white supremacy*, they imagine white robes and burning crosses, but not the subtle ways in which Black and brown people are talked about and treated.[10] They cannot see that in professional contexts such as academia, religious institutions, and corporations, advancement is given to those who meet certain "requirements" and not to others. They cannot see how their speech and actions contribute to further hurt and inequalities for others.

I once taught in a seemingly very progressive philosophy department, which employed a gay instructor as well as three women, two of whom were Latina, within a department so small that it had to be joined with the psychology department. Before my friend resigned from the school, she helped me obtain part-time work there. Adding me to their teaching roster seemed to advance their agenda of "diversity." But outside my office was a hallway where the photographs of the entire department hung; the majority were white and male. When there was an opportunity for full-time employment, my female colleagues all urged me to apply for the position. When I talked to the director, I found out that a white male candidate was already being considered even before the job had been posted. I was qualified for the position and had published an adequate number of academic articles, but the director already knew who he had in mind for the position, and another pale-skinned male was added to the wall of whiteness.

This is the point of racism: Racism involves believing that only certain people are meant to do certain things, and then acting on this belief. Racism does not only involve saying, "I hate such-and-such people." It is much more subtle than that. Racism leads a director to cast non-Vietnamese actors to play the major roles in *Miss Saigon*, even when there are many qualified Vietnamese actors, as occurred in Houston, home to the country's third largest Vietnamese population. While a Filipino actor can arguably play a Vietnamese character, engaging the language and singing it is a different matter, and something that many Vietnamese actors would be well-qualified to do. This subtle form of racism results in seeing people as qualified to fill only certain roles. Camara Jones, a physician and civil rights activist, provides a definition of racism that is extremely helpful. Racism, Jones says, is "a system of structuring opportunity and assigning value based on the social interpretation of how one looks"[11] (what we call "race").

In my university department, I was *valued* because I added to the "diversity" of the department, but I was not valued per se as an instructor. I was not given the *opportunity* to advance, similarly to some of my female colleagues who did not receive tenure. Those making these decisions were not uneducated backwoods people; they were highly educated liberals who were unable to see their own blind spots. Whether progressive or conservative, I've encountered similar hallways on many academic campuses and in many institutions of learning. Racial bias seems to be built into the system. These constructs continue to exist among white Americans who do not want to embrace their histories and accept the reality of the racial injustices and inequities that presently exist.

THE LIBERATING IMAGE OF GOD

In the first creation story of Genesis, we find these words:

> Therefore, God created humankind in God's image,
>> in the image of God created them;
>> male and female God created them.
>> (Genesis 1:27, translation mine)[12]

If Christians believe that we are all made in the image of God, shouldn't that belief provide the premise for all our human relations and interactions? Many of the Eastern fathers believed that humanity did not "fall" from grace, but simply lacked the maturity to realize their full potential as God's image bearers. Thinkers like Irenaeus attributed Adam and Eve's disobedience more to a developmental error than to direct human intent. Because humanity was immature, we lacked the ability to truly make the choices that were best for us. We were responsible for our actions, but our actions came from a state in which we were not fully formed into the image that God intended us to bear. As a result, we were deceived, and our natures were taken captive. The incarnation of God provided a way for humanity's full nature to be restored.

Augustine, who believed that the image of God in us was heavily damaged by sin, was not as optimistic. John Calvin was even more pessimistic in his theological anthropology, believing humans to be so marred by sin that they do not have the free will to make choices, and it therefore is entirely up to God to provide a will that will allow humans to choose God. "Total depravity" is closely associated with predestination in Calvin's thought and in his belief system, which developed into Calvinism.

Philosophically, this corresponds to Thomas Hobbes's view that humans are by nature selfish and cruel people. In his famous book *Leviathan*, Hobbes (1588–1679) describes human life as "solitary, poor, nasty, brutish and short." Hobbes held that only an absolute monarchy was able to tame human nature so that society could operate. The government he described was not a government "for the people and by the people," but a government against the people.

The more depraved that people are perceived to be, the more they need to be controlled. Total depravity requires that God become the sole sovereign of goodness who needs to save humans from their wickedness. This way of perceiving God's relationship to humanity is not a viable option, because it provides a passive view of human actions and the consequences of our actions toward other people, and it fails to take into account the totality of human nature. To use Alasdair MacIntyre's definition, people, by nature, are not only rational animals, but dependent ones.[13] We are not created as individual separate and solitary creatures, but are created to be connected to family, friends, society, and other organizations. Therefore, the image of God that is in us is dependent and relational. To synthesize views of the Eastern fathers and MacIntyre, we might say that humans are good by nature, but our goodness needs to be developed in relationship to God, others, and this universe.

The further one moves from the view that humans, by nature, are intrinsically good and made in the image of God, the greater the distrust of people and the need to tightly govern people. In our cultural fabric, we have determined which people are "good" and "evil" through racialization. Consider how television shows and movies depict Black men in comparison to white men. If a young Black man uses drugs or belongs to a gang, the show is likely one about criminal investigations, such as *Law and Order*. But when a white male is depicted using drugs, molesting women, or participating in a gang at his college—otherwise known as a fraternity—the show is most likely a situation comedy about frat boys having a good time and acting crazy. The cold truth is that 11.2 percent of college women (one in ten) report assault or rape by men,[14] while 21.3 percent of male college students (one in five) report using illegal drugs monthly.[15] White college students are not targeted for prosecution of these crimes, and those who are caught are not sentenced as severely as Black males prosecuted for the same crimes.[16] Fraternities have their own "gang signs" and wear their own gang-specific apparel, and many participate in acts of violence and human abuse in the form of hazing.[17] However, they are given a pass, and their indiscretions are not the focus of society-wide fear and hate. Instead, laws such as the "stop and frisk" policy create ways to target Black men, who are deemed "bad" by society.[18]

The more viable approach to human nature is the perspective that we all, by *essence*, are made in the image of God, but that we often *exist* as people who are sometimes good and sometimes bad. This is not merely a philosophical distinction, but represents a real difference. This is the way we normally view the behavior of other nonhuman animals.

When I adopted my dog and cats, I did not do so with the belief that they were morally depraved animals. Rather, they are creatures who need training. When they do something that I do not like, such as when my dog, Blondie, took a bite out of my *Collected Works of Plato*, I say "Bad girl" and scold her, but I do not believe that she is, by nature, a bad creature. She *did* something bad mainly because I had not trained her not to do it. Socrates, in *The Apology*, argues that one can shape morality through appropriate pedagogy (although Blondie may believe otherwise!).

The Eastern fathers described this type of training and "growing into" God's perfection by using the language of the image of God. Clement of Alexandria (c. 150–c. 215) compared the Law of Moses to Greek philosophy, arguing that just as philosophy serves as a custodian or teacher (Greek *epaidagogei*), so the Law of Moses serves as a guide in preparing humanity "for its perfection in Christ."[19] Irenaeus of Lyons describes all humanity as children of God who are also separated from God because of disobedience.[20] He uses the image of a child's inheritance to describe the image of God within humans, arguing that a child can be disinherited and not receive their parent's property, but the child remains a daughter or son. In the same way, people may become alienated from God, yet remain children of God. We may act badly, even while we remain made in the image of God. As noted, human restoration takes place through what Irenaeus calls "recapitulation," or a reframing of history in which Christ undoes the actions of Adam that intro-duced death into the world. Jesus takes away death through his defeat of death and the evil systems of the universe. Irenaeus believed that God did not arbitrarily create some people bad and others good, but gave humans agency and the ability to choose between right and wrong, good and evil.[21] Christ's work was to help us mature in order to perform those appropriate, godlike actions.

Both of these theological frameworks include a type of leading and instruction that assists humans in achieving their fullest potential. In restoring the image of God in humans, God liberates the image of God within us, making our fullest flourishing possible. Just as eliminating evil is not a one-time event, so freeing the image of God within humanity is not a sudden, single act. It occurs through God's empowerment of humans in an ongoing relationship throughout a person's lifetime.

Hebrew scholar J. Richard Middleton describes the *imago Dei* as the "liberating image." In his discussion of Genesis 1 and the image of God, Middleton concludes: "In the end, the liberating character of the *imago Dei* is grounded in the nature of God, who calls the world into being as an act of generosity. This means that we cannot artificially separate our vision of God's redemptive love from an understanding of God's creative power. A careful reading of Genesis 1:1–2:3 thus converges on John 3:16. In both creation and redemption, 'God so loved the world that he gave . . .'"[22]

The liberating image of God within humanity is a generous outpouring of God's nature. God is powerful because God works to *empower* God's creation. God's power involves cooperation between God, humans, and all of creation. The image of God that is reflected in humans is an example of the overflowing abundance in creation. This image helps us to see ourselves in relationship with all the world and also prompts us to help others see their own image of God.

The writer of James makes a searing accusation concerning speech marked by hypocritical piety: "With it we bless the Lord and Father, and with it we curse those who are made in the likeness of God" (James 3:9). Activist Lisa Sharon Harper writes in *The Very Good Gospel* that the description of humans as made in the image of God in Genesis was intended by its authors to restore the sense of agency that Israel lost during exile and captivity in Babylon. This claim that the image of God is within all humans was countercultural in the original context of Genesis, in which women were considered property. Harper argues that in claiming that the image of God is reflected in all humans, as expressed in Genesis 1:27, the writers of Scripture "declare that both men and women are made in the image of God. Both men and women are born with inherent dignity and worth. Women bear the image of God equally, with no distinction in the way that image is manifest."[23]

When we proclaim that people are made in the very image and likeness of God, we are affirming that we have shared agency and humanity. Those made in the image of God are like us. And when we empower people to obtain agency and recognize their humanity, we enable that same image of God in ourselves. We become more restored because we are, by nature, connected to others. This is how we participate in God's work of liberating creation from the bonds that we have imposed by our dehumanizing efforts to subjugate and racialize people.

Some people, at times, are not able to realize and accept this liberation. Their own internal bondage may be too great. When this is the case, we need to pray for them. By praying for our "enemies," we make them into our friends. Such people may continue to bury the image of the divine within themselves under selfishness and blame, and may never really become our friends. However, prayer reminds us of our interdependent connection to each other and that we are

not isolated individuals, but creatures tied together by a divine web
as fellow image bearers.

JESUS AND THE IMAGE OF GOD

Jesus saw himself in the people he served. Although others called
him "the messiah" (Hebrew *ha mashiach*) or "the Christ" (Greek
ho christos), he called himself "the Son of Humanity" (Hebrew *ben
adam*). This image comes from the Hebrew prophet Daniel, who
describes one who is "like a son of man" (Daniel 7:13) who is given
dominion and kingship over the nations of the earth. This title is
one of both authority and solidarity. Jesus, as the Son of Man, is
submerged in the waters of the Jordan in order to bring people from
one nation to another, from one kingdom to another.

Bible scholar Bob Ekblad imaginatively interprets Jesus as the
Buen Coyote (the Good Coyote) who smuggles us to freedom from
our captors and delivers us into a new kingdom.[24] Restoration starts
with liberation. The Jewish Passover feast re-creates the drama of
deliverance. The synoptic gospels (Matthew, Mark, and Luke) depict
the Last Supper in terms of the Passover, or paschal, meal. Some elements of the meal are not described in detail, such as the eating of
the paschal lamb, which seems to indicate that Jesus was pointing
not toward the passing of the Angel of Death but toward the hurried
way in which the Jews prepared to leave Egypt, so quickly that they
did not have time to let the yeast rise in their bread. Jesus reinter-
prets the Passover, portraying it as a story of deliverance rather than
one of vengeance.[25] Similarly, the cup and the bread point toward
the self-sacrifice of Jesus and not toward the "sacrifice for" aspect of
the Passover meal. Jesus is not saying that God needs a sacrifice in
order to free us; he is saying that God does free us, and this freedom
involves a self-giving of God. This is a subtle but immense difference.

But deliverance is not only from places, from nation to God's
kingdom or from Egypt to the Promised Land. Deliverance

involves our entire being, how we perceive and live in our universe. Philosophically speaking, to change the form of something is to change its purpose, its intended goal. If I put a hole in a cup, the form changes, and it no longer serves its purpose as a cup. If I recycle the cup and it becomes a plate, its purpose changes again. When the image of God is restored in us, we become who we are intended to be, and we are enabled to do what we are intended to do in the world. Jesus' work in the world was to restore the *imago Dei* in each of us so that we might live in ways that bring life and meaning throughout this world. The purpose of restoration is to make us like God (not God, but *like* God), a process that the Eastern fathers called *theosis*.

Theosis involves bringing our nature into union with God's nature. Through theosis, the image of God within us is restored by making us like God. However, a continual holding on to a mentality of scarcity, of not-enough-ness, keeps us holding on to what we perceive to be our most cherished belongings—our land, our possessions, ourselves—and keeps us from this divine likeness. We cannot let go, and therefore we cannot be transformed. The most privileged people in the United States are those who fight the most for power and position because they are most afraid to lose it, and because they believe that there isn't enough of it to go around. God is not afraid of losing any of these things, because God is all and encompasses all within God's being. The more that we are like God, the more we can let go of our perception of scarcity.

To summarize, there are several aspects to how we see ourselves:

- As created in the likeness and image of God
- In the process of being transformed so that we can manifest God's image more fully and empower others to see themselves as image bearers as well

- In the process of being unified with the divine nature so that our image can look like the image of God, a process known as *theosis*

In the next chapter, I will discuss one of the most pervasive myths in Christianity that has kept this system of scarcity in play and has even been offered as a solution to the problem of sin in this world. This is the penal substitutionary view of atonement. Rather than rehashing all the theological debates around atonement theories (since this has been done better elsewhere), I will discuss what these ideas mean in our world and how they have shaped our culture in the West.[26] This particular view has caused more injustice and problems than it attempts to solve.

Theosis

The idea presented by the Eastern fathers that humans can grow into the likeness of God. This is also known as divinization, in which people are restored to their original human nature and become united to the divine. In the early Eastern church this was expressed through Athanasius's famous statement, "The Word of God became human so that humans can become more like God."

5

HEALING FROM THE DEPTHS OF WOUNDEDNESS

If the God of Jesus' cross is found among the least, the crucified people of the world, then God is also found among those lynched in American history.

—JAMES CONE, *The Cross and the Lynching Tree*

He is sentenced by the religious leaders of his day, the gatekeepers of the faith. The same men who spoke of the loving-kindness of YHWH God have accused him of blasphemy. They charge him with maligning God's good name, with doing miracles and casting out demons through the power of demons. They accuse him of abandoning the cherished traditions and laws—traditions and laws that neglected the poor and sick. These men offer him to the Roman courts to be executed.

He offers them something better. He offers them love and a way of life that will unburden them and give them ultimate happiness. They think they have everything they need. They are comfortable with the Roman occupation and the religious status quo. Just as animals in captivity may not recognize their cages, they do not see the prison surrounding them.

The soldiers, rather than welcoming him as a liberating king, beat him. They mock him and strip him naked. He is strung up before the world to see. The soldiers write a scornful inscription, "King of the Jews," above the cross to which he is nailed, and weave a crown of thorns as a symbol of their derision. They hang him beside thieves and insurrectionists because the verdict at his trial is treason. His people declare him king, even though by law there is no king but Caesar. He stood against the tide of Roman nationalism and now is swept under by its current of violence and hatred.

He is abandoned by most of his male disciples, who leave him alone at the cross. The women stand by him, weeping for him, and will bury him. Others betray him and leave him to die alone. The pain of loving the world is great, too great even for him. Love breaks him, breaks him into pieces. He does not want to be in this place in his journey. He is caught in impending suffering and the consequences of his actions, his heart torn in two. At the Mount of Olives, he poured out a prayer for deliverance from this turmoil. His tears and sweat poured out onto the ground, like blood draining from his body.

High up on the cross, even with blood dripping into his eyes, he can see everyone, including mourners and scoffers. He turns his eyes upward to see if God is there but is met only with a looming dark sky. He prays a psalm of the abandoned, striking at the hearts of those who gave him up to this punishment and as a reminder of God's vindication. And then he asks that his Father forgive those who crucified him for their ignorance. He gazes down on the world and his people. He breathes one last time, a painful breath unlike the one with which he had come into the world.

Darkness and death.

Darkness.

DID GOD DO IT?

What if I asked you out for a brunch date—I'll cook, as I often do, and you can bring the ingredients? We decide on omelets for the menu. So you come over with groceries, including a carton of eggs. As you step into the kitchen, I trip you. You hit the ground, the bag falls onto the floor, and the eggs break.

You exclaim, "Why did you do that?!"

"You can't make an omelet without breaking a few eggs," I reply snarkily.

What if I did the same thing every time you brought over groceries? What would you think of me?

"I'd think you were a jerk" replied a member of a church audience when I asked this question.

Many Christians have come to think of this as the image of a loving God. This image has been propagated in Western Christianity through what is known as the penal substitutionary view of atonement. This view holds that God *had* to sacrifice Jesus on the cross in order to save humanity from their sins and spare them from eternal punishment, and argues that God could not do otherwise because there was no other way. Either humanity would perish or God's only Son would perish. Because God chose God's Son to perish, this behavior must be love. But is it really love? If so, love of whom?

How can we trust a God who behaves in this way? More importantly, how is this God any different from someone who does evil? Pastor and author John Piper goes so far as to say that God ordains bad things to happen.[1] When a natural disaster strikes and kills people, such as the three thousand people in Puerta Rico killed by Hurricane Maria, Piper said it was God's doing. When a baby dies in the hospital, that is God's doing. When a shooter guns down students at a school—yep, entirely God. People advocating this theory claim that God ordains evil for a divine purpose, often one that we cannot see.

I've heard many Christians theologize about suffering by saying, "It's okay. God did it for a reason." Statements like these bring more hurt into the world than they relieve. Such comments indicate: "It's okay that we do bad things. It's okay that we are not mindful of our actions. It's okay that we hurt others. God will use it." The apostle Paul writes to the church in Rome, "And why not say (as some people slander us by saying that we say), 'Let us do evil so that good may come'?" (Romans 3:8), indicating that some people were likely accusing Christians of claiming this degree of freedom. But if God is all powerful and all creative, then why does God need to do evil in order to accomplish good? Why does God need to trip you in order to make omelets? Why doesn't God just make omelets? (Trust me, they are not that hard to make.)

At a breakfast for chaplains, the president of a Christian university told the story of Phan Thị Kim Phúc, a Vietnamese girl who appeared in a world-famous photograph as she ran naked from a napalm bombing when she was only nine years old. Kim Phúc and her family were living in the village of Trảng Bàng, a town that was attacked and occupied by the North Vietnamese Army. Kim Phúc fled the town along with others, but South Vietnamese planes mistook her group for North Army soldiers and rained down napalm on the villagers. She suffered third-degree burns down her back and was forced to remove her clothing as she fled because it was on fire. Kim Phúc and her family eventually moved to Canada, where she became a citizen and converted to the Christian faith, which helped her to cope with the physical and emotional trauma of her wounds. The president of this university told the story of Kim

Phúc's conversion in an attempt to ease the horrors of the Vietnam War. "If this war did not happen," he reasoned, "then Kim Phúc would not have become a Christian." I was horrified by this interpretation of events.

Did God kill fifty-eight thousand U.S. soldiers and over two million Vietnamese men, women, and children in order for this woman to believe in God? Was there no other way? This logic (or lack thereof) reveals why there seems to be no resistance to war in the United States. In this view, humans are simply cannon fodder that God uses to make Christians. Only the simplicity of the human mind could think of God in this way. The philosopher David Hume calls this the *post hoc, ergo propter hoc* fallacy (Latin: after this, therefore because of this). If I wash my car, and then it rains, I might conclude, "Every time I wash my car it rains." I begin to believe there is a meteorological conspiracy against me, preventing me from having a clean car. I don't think, "I normally wash my car at times when it has not rained recently. But on days when there has been no rain for a while, it is more likely to rain, so it is likely to rain on days when I wash my car." That would be reasonable. Most people don't *actually* believe the car wash–rain fallacy to be true. They just *pretend* to believe it is true. Like all kinds of superstitions, we want it to be true because life would be that much simpler if it were.

This is the way that many Christians and other theists think about God. They reason that God orchestrated an event, planned it out, made it happen, so that the result could occur in a particular way. Then they conclude, "Everything happens for a reason." This is simplistic thinking. It is more difficult to face the reality that some bad things happen simply because they are the *result* of bad actions, and that some bad things just happen, period. There is sometimes no reason behind it.

One of my philosophy professors in graduate school explained this to me through a simple illustration. Let's imagine that a very cruel person took you hostage and locked you up in a room. You are bound to a chair, a gun is put to your head, and you are threatened with being shot. A deck of cards is in front of you. Your captor gives you a chance to escape if you choose the queen of hearts. Your captor shuffles the deck and gives you a chance to pick one card. You hesitantly draw a card, which turns out to be the correct one. You escape horrific doom. As a result, you determine, "This must be fate. What are the chances?" The chances are actually one in fifty-two, but you are amazed, and conclude that this must be God's work. Whether God helped you out or not is not the point. The point is that if you chose wrongly, you would not know otherwise. You would be dead, and that would be the end of the story.

This is how events in our world occur. Events happen, and because they did *not* happen differently, we do not know otherwise. This does not mean that they are meant to be or that God orchestrated events to occur in this way. God could help you out and God could do things to intervene. And often God does bring out good from evil; this is God's nature. However, this reasoning does not work the other way around. God does not do evil *so that* good can occur. How do I know this? If I believe in a God who is involved in people's lives, an engaged God, then why would God need to do that? To teach us something? To make a point? If that is the case, I don't really know the point.

It makes more sense and is more consistent with how God works in the world, and is more consistent with the life of Jesus, to simply say that God does good. God is love. God is goodness. God is redemptive. When we put away any notions that God needs to do evil so that good can come out of it, we become more compassionate and empathetic to the problems of people. Yes, good *can* come out of bad situations, but not all things that come out of bad situations are good. To call something good when it is wrong, bad, or evil is to have a wrongheaded view of the world. Making such a claim itself is wrong, bad, and evil. Doing so perpetuates evil and injustice instead of preventing it. Would we want more bad things to happen in our lives so that "good" things can arise? There are very few steps in logic between saying "Things happen for a reason" and saying "Let's do evil so that good things can come out of it." Such an approach is one of masochism, receiving pleasure from punishment. Rather, we ought to seek to prevent evil and to limit the hurt that we deal out to this world.

CRIME AND PUNISHMENT

I once asked a former death row inmate, Anthony Graves, to meet me for lunch. I'd had the pleasure of introducing him at a conference the week before, and wanted to talk with him about his work with his nonprofit foundation.[2] In 1992, Graves was misidentified as the person who murdered six people in Summerville, Texas, not far from where Graves worked in Austin. Despite a series of incompetent attorneys, Graves finally found a lawyer to appeal his case and was exonerated. Graves told me that he is the 138th death row exoneree—a number, he concluded, that was too high, because every exoneree represents a person who was unjustly sentenced in the first place. Unfortunately, Graves will almost certainly not be the last to be exonerated.

Our penal system incarcerates a disproportionate number of people of color, and places some on death row for crimes they did not commit. This is a system that many are willing to live with because life moves on for most people in the United States. They are not at risk for being targeted, incarcerated, or put on death row. Still, while the U.S. population represents about 4.5 percent of the world's population, the number of people incarcerated in the United States represents around 22 percent of incarcerated people worldwide. How did we come to see incarceration as a solution to our society's problems?

Historian Timothy Gorringe has a convincing theory that speaks of the powerful force of religion in culture. Gorringe's thesis is this: Because Christian theology was an important part of Western society until the nineteenth century, theologies of atonement, and particularly penal substitutionary atonement, became pervasive to the point that they influenced the criminal justice system, linking the notion of sin with crime.[3]

Penal substitutionary atonement involves several technical terms:

- *Penal* – Relating to penalty and punishment. We talk about our prison system as a penal system.
- *Substitution* – To replace one with another.
- *Atonement* – A Latin word that means to make right. It is used to translate the Hebrew word *kippur*, as in the Day of Atonement (Yom Kippur), in which bulls and rams were sacrificed to expunge the sins of Israel. This term has been used to describe what happened in Jesus' death on the cross.

The penal substitutionary view of atonement is often expressed as including the following arguments:

- God is angry because of sin.
- God's anger is directed at humanity because of this sin.
- To divert God's wrath, a substitute must be punished instead.
- In the Hebrew Scriptures, an animal is used to divert God's wrath.
- The animal is sacrificed, and God's wrath is poured out on this animal instead of on humans.
- This was an annual offering, but Jesus' death became the final offering, making further animal offerings unnecessary. In

Jesus' death, once and for all, all sins were taken care of on the cross, which served as the sacrificial altar of God.

- If you believe in Jesus' substitutionary atonement on the cross, then you will be spared from damnation. If you do not, then God's wrath is still upon you.

This view was thoroughly developed by Anselm of Canterbury in the eleventh century and further articulated by John Calvin in the sixteenth century. Anselm was a logician at heart, and his tight logic is visible in the premises and conclusions of this argument. Drawing on the concept of a nobleman's honor in the feudal Middle Ages, Anselm understood sin to be an offense against God's honor, which humans were required to restore. Calvin used legal terminology to describe the injustice done to God because of sin, which Calvin defined as a violation of God's law. I will not attempt to be exhaustive here in my arguments against penal substitutionary atonement,[4] but I do want to show *how* these arguments can lead to where we are as a society, especially in the West.

Like many Christians, especially in the United States, I encountered these ideas when I became a Christian, even though I was moved to faith not by the notion that I was a sinner, but by Jesus' Sermon on the Mount. Nevertheless, this view of atonement is often the entry point to Christianity in the West, a gateway for other Christian beliefs. If one does not assent to the conditions of this argument, then it often seems that one cannot believe anything else about Christianity.

The problem with the logic of Anselm and Calvin is not in the framing of their arguments or in their use of logic. Arguments are as good as the accuracy of their premises. I may have a perfectly valid argument but still have a false conclusion. If my premises are false, my conclusions must be false. Consider this argument:

If the moon is made of green cheese, then there are mice on the moon.

The moon is made of green cheese.

Therefore, there are mice on the moon.

This is what logicians call a valid argument. It is valid because the structure of the argument is consistent with the rules of logic. *If* the premises are true, then the conclusion *must be true*. However, I said *if*. So if the premise that the moon is made of green cheese is true, and I follow this structure, then the conclusion of the argument is true.

A valid argument is like a set of approved architectural plans. An architect can draw plans for a house, but the plans must be approved by an engineer to demonstrate that the building plan will work in the real world. What if I build my house based loosely on the approved plans, but use paper rather than wood, bricks, and sheetrock? That would be ridiculous. The house would fall apart. It would not be a *sound* structure.

In the same way, an argument can be valid but not sound. Are all the statements in the argument true, really true? Or are they made of cheese?

Consider the first assertion of the penal substitutionary atonement argument: God is angry at humanity because of sin. *Is* God angry because of sin? Does sin keep God away from us, or does it keep us away from God? A bounty of passages in the Hebrew Scriptures talk about God's forgiveness of sin without talking about a need for sacrificial punishment:

> Blessed is the one
>> whose transgressions are forgiven,
>> whose sins are covered.
> Blessed is the one
>> whose sin the LORD does not count against them
>> and in whose spirit is no deceit. (Psalm 32:1-2 NIV)

"Forgive the iniquity of this people according to the greatness of your steadfast love, just as you have pardoned this people, from Egypt even until now."

Then the Lord said, "I do forgive, just as you have asked." (Numbers 14:19-20)

Wash me thoroughly from my iniquity,
　　and cleanse me from my sin. . . .
Purge me with hyssop, and I shall be clean;
　　wash me, and I shall be whiter than snow. (Psalm 51:2, 7)

The Lord is merciful and gracious,
　　slow to anger and abounding in steadfast love.
He will not always accuse,
　　nor will he keep his anger forever.
He does not deal with us according to our sins,
　　nor repay us according to our iniquities.
For as the heavens are high above the earth,
　　so great is his steadfast love toward those who fear him;
as far as the east is from the west,
　　so far he removes our transgressions from us.
　　(Psalm 103:8-12)

The list goes on.

If God forgave in the Old Testament, why could God not simply forgive in the same way in the New Testament? Was Jesus not able to "look upon" sin? He was accused of hanging out with the "sinners," of eating and drinking with them. The incident when he expressed anger involved the desecration of the temple, which he considered to be his Father's house. The temple was not where the "sinners" were, but where the religious people had set up a concession stand to sell offerings to appease God. They turned the sacrificial system into a religious monopoly and moneymaker. In actuality, the sacrificial system was not about appeasing the wrath of God, but about appeasing the wrath of people. The temple had been turned into a den of thieves and robbers. The sin that angered Jesus was about the injustices against his people, the oppressed, the suffering. Even so, he was able to deal with those who caused offense without calling down fire from heaven. He confronted people without inflicting violence on them. God can deal with sin in a way that does not need to involve the condemnation of all humanity to hell.

Hell and damnation, wrath and punishment, are not necessities for an all-loving, just, and holy God. Instead, they appear to make a mockery of God. Sin does not thwart God's love and involvement with us, but it becomes a problem when it gets in the way of our connection with God and others, when we do wrong to the divine image in others. The medieval theologian Thomas Aquinas reasoned that if damnation and death were the only way for God to deal with sin, God's hand would be forced—and who can force God's hand?[5] God is not bound by these rules, but because the crucifixion did happen and Jesus did die, God worked through these events to redeem humanity. God made the best of what humanity dished out. Historically, this has always been the case.

If God's anger was not appeased on the cross, then what did happen there? The theologians who wrote the New Testament had little to say about this. Even Paul is vague about what Jesus' death meant, and theologians and scholars debate ad infinitum the passages that address it (Romans 3:21-26; Galatians 2:19-20). The writer of the gospel of Mark uses imagery as a way of interpretation (Mark 15:38). There, the evangelist describes the curtain in the temple's innermost sanctum, the holy of holies, being torn from top to bottom. Only a priest could enter the holy of holies, and only one time a year, on Yom Kippur. How did the writer know that this event happened on the day Jesus died? There was no way someone could have reported this to him, because it's very unlikely that someone who knew that Jesus died at that very moment was also present to observe the tearing of the curtain. There was no live breaking news broadcast of the crucifixion to reach viewers at the temple. But Mark's description of the tearing of the curtain was a way to *describe* a theological event. It symbolizes the breaking of the barrier between God and humanity in the event of the crucifixion. This act demonstrated that there is no separation, no holy other, in the man of Christ. He was vulnerable to death, and God died in the moment when humanity killed God. The imagery is powerful.

We are free to interpret the events of the cross. There is no systematic theology within Scripture that explicitly shows *how* God redeemed humanity; Scripture simply reports what happened and the results. This leads me to my next point about penal substitution.

VIOLENCE AS A SOLUTION

The main strategy for solving problems of conflict and difference in the United States is through violence. Anthropologist René Girard and scholar William James have labeled the beliefs underlying this approach "the myth of sanctioned violence."[6] Theologian Walter Wink calls it "the myth of redemptive violence."[7] This violence may occur in the form of psychological, physical, or social harm done to others. Verbal threats and intimidation against those whose views differ litter social media. The United States was born of violent revolution and civil strife. Deep in this country's subconscious, we believe that the use of force and death can resolve problems, and that this strategy is ordained by God and therefore must be correct. There is a tightly held belief that God uses violence *in order to* redeem humanity from their sins. This view is implicit in the ways in which redemption is often talked about among evangelicals and other Christians, especially in the West. God does harm to X in order to achieve purposes Y. The reasoning also seems to be contradictory when applied to something like extremist Islamic fundamentalists. People are perceived as evil when strapping bombs to themselves and killing many others in the name of Allah, but God is *not* seen as evil in killing God's Son to solve the problem of sin for humanity. It is easier to perceive evil in others than to see the flaws in one's own system of thought.

The problem of sanctioned violence comes in the form of penal substitution. I am not critical of the understanding of *substitutionary* atonement. I see evidence of substitution in the Bible and in the ways that we often interact with one another. We make sacrifices all the time on behalf of people whom we love, and even on behalf of those we do not know. A soldier falls on a grenade for her comrades. A mother sacrifices her career for her family. To save others or a relationship, a person will claim that a disagreement was her fault even though it was not. However, would it be just and right if a person were *forced* to do this?

Consider this example. I see that one of my students is struggling in a class. She is constantly failing the exams. But another student is doing very well, so one day I decide to *substitute* the failing student's exams for the grade of the student who is receiving an A in my class. One student did the work, studied hard, and showed up, and that student's grade is used to make up for the grade of the failing student. I file my grades with the school registrar, making them final. Someone needed to fail because someone did not do well. It would not be "just" if both of the students received As, because only one student did the hard work. One student *had* to be punished. This is the logic of penal substitutionary atonement. The emphasis is on forcing one person to receive the punishment for another in order to atone for my wrath as a professor and therefore move my anger away from one student and onto the other. This is what theologians call "propitiation," or satisfying the wrath of God.

In what world would this be a just system? In all places, and all situations, this rationale would be considered unjust and wrong, so why is it upheld in a system of Christian thought? Because some believe that this is God's rationale, we think it must be correct. But this is not God's way of thinking (and I'm not claiming I know God's way of thinking); it is simply an *interpretation* of what happened at the cross that is made by some Christian theologians. This interpretation is neither explicit in the Bible nor part of the teachings of Jesus or the early church, and especially not of the Eastern fathers. As I explained in chapter 3, the early Eastern fathers argued for no such plan of salvation. They saw that people needed to grow into their true selves, understood that sin had made people sick, both spiritually and physically, and believed that people needed healing and liberation.

As discussed, Irenaeus of Lyons proposed the idea of recapitulation. Recapitulation was a way to summarize a theme or narrative (from the Latin *capitula*: head or chapter). Irenaeus saw that Christ had summed up all of history in a way that retold the history that had been written by the first man, Adam:

> God has therefore, in God's work of recapitulation, summed up all things, both waging war against our enemy, and crushing him who had at the beginning led us away captives in Adam, and trampled upon his head, as you can perceive in Genesis that God said to the serpent, "And I will put enmity between you and the woman, and between your seed and her seed; He shall be on the watch for your head, and you on the watch for His heel."[8]

Adam brought death and sin into the world, but Christ brought life and redemption. In this way, Jesus rewrites the story of our lives. We are not fated to face the shame of sin and death as did our forefather—the representative human, Adam—but to live a new life. The story of Jesus reframes and reformats the story of Adam.

Jesus' existence is a storied existence, one of struggle and victory. This narrative of Jesus' life is painfully absent from the penal substitutionary view of atonement. I often ask my students, "If Jesus' only mission was to die on the cross to save the sins of the world, then why didn't someone simply plunge a knife into the baby Jesus? Why the thirty years of hardship? Why the ministry and miracles? Why the teachings and the stories? If we are just to believe an 'idea,' why not just kill baby Jesus and ask us to recite a mantra of believing 'that Jesus died for our sins'?" But if we consider the entire life of Jesus, his birth, his growing up, his pimples and awkward puberty, his struggles against temptation, and his existential life crises, his pain over loving people, and his betrayal by some of those same people, and the hope that flowers from his death, then we have a narrative that we can relate to and identify with. His story can be our story, and our stories can be his stories. We can make some sense of our life and of his.

This should be a liberating narrative for many of us. This narrative declares that God has put an end to the history of death and the sin that results. We do not have to repeat the same mistakes of our parental figures and can write a new narrative. But the question is, Does this happen? Is this really the case? I would argue that we do not have to and cannot wait until Christ returns to make this a reality. In other words, the realization that this has not happened means that there is more to say about the story of redemption, that the defeat of Satan and of systemic and structural evils have to take place in this new world.

HEALING THROUGH HIS WOUNDS

Scripture scholar Bob Ekblad spends his days reading the Bible "with the damned"[9]—those who have been condemned by our society, including people who are formerly incarcerated, who are drug addicted, or who are immigrants. We condemn them because they represent those parts of ourselves that we cannot bear to look at. They speak of our greatest need and desire. But because we often struggle to look at ourselves honestly, these people have to be "damned." They suffer because many are not willing to admit that we "need" to have these people in order to maintain relative peace with one another.

In her short story "The Ones Who Walk Away from Omelas," Ursula K. Le Guin depicts a fictional utopian town that prospers through the suffering of a single child. The people in this town are happy and enjoy the pleasures of food, sex, and even recreational drugs. "Joyous! How is one to tell about joy? How describe the citizens of Omelas?" writes the narrator.

But the reader is introduced to a horrible surprise. In the basement of one of Omelas's beautiful buildings is a child. "It might be a boy or a girl. It looks about six, but actually is nearly ten. It is feebleminded. Perhaps it was born defective, or perhaps it has become imbecile through fear, malnutrition, and neglect. It picks its nose and occasionally fumbles vaguely with its toes or genitals, as it sits hunched in the corner farthest from the bucket and the two mops."[10]

The child has been locked up in the cellar of this building, barely fed, not clothed, left to sit naked in its own excrement. The people of Omelas know the child is there, and some have even visited it. But most are content that because of this child the citizens of Omelas can enjoy their life. Some young people see the child and are horrified and distraught by the sight. But they understand clearly the terms of their society. If the child is taken out of its prison, is clothed, fed, and treated kindly, their society will disappear. They justify their passivity by wondering what benefit it would provide the child to be treated decently. Would the child even know and appreciate the difference?

Le Guin's town is not very different from many situations we find in our society. Some of us see and recognize the cruelty that exists. Some of us see the scapegoats in the prison systems, in the large disparities and inequities between rich and poor, in the ways that people of color and immigrants are scapegoated, but we would rather not disrupt the systems that keep us happy.

The economic crisis of 2008 was caused by people on Wall Street, mainly white business professionals, who were obsessively greedy. This financial crisis cost Americans $12.8 trillion. That is trillion dollars—not billions, but trillions![11] The U.S. Department of Justice only arrested and prosecuted one Wall Street executive, Kareem Serageldin, who had tried to hide $100 million in losses, just 0.0000078125 percent of the financial losses of the entire crisis. Out of all the financial executives who were involved, only the Egyptian-born Serageldin was arrested and sentenced to thirty months in federal prison. We can easily see the scapegoats in our society.

Anthropologist René Girard writes about the "scapegoat mechanism," a theory that explains how societies use scapegoats. It starts with what he calls "mimetic desire," or the need to imitate others in our society. I use this example in the classroom: Let's say that you were the most popular and pretty girl in high school and your family had wealth and ample resources. But there was another girl who was also popular and pretty. She could be your rival and enemy. She could take away all your fame, which, for you, translates into power. But instead of making her your enemy, you befriend her and form a truce. However, for the friendship to last, you need someone whom both of you can despise and ridicule. Together, you pick the girl who is, in your minds, the ugliest, weakest, and most vulnerable girl. By choosing this girl as the object of your spite, the two of you have become friends and your bond is sealed. Your rivalry against each other is taken out on an innocent scapegoat.

Girard argues that this is how society works. We choose an innocent victim or victims and blame them for the woes of society. This blaming might appear in the form of blaming the "witches" of Salem for epileptic seizures suffered by young girls in the 1690s. This could appear as blaming the Jews of Germany for the economic crisis of the 1920s. It could take the form of blaming immigrants instead of technological advancements for the loss of jobs in the

2000s. It could appear as the branding and banning of Muslims from entering the country out of fear that they will commit terrorism on American soil. If there is someone to blame, then society can stay intact.

When this theory is applied in a religious context, it is called "the myth of sanctioned violence." Jesus is taken out of the city gates to be crucified, and this is given sanction by the religious order: "Cursed is everyone who hangs on a tree" (Galatians 3:13, paraphrasing Deuteronomy 21:22-23). The Roman tetrarch Pontius Pilate and the Jewish governor King Herod, who once were enemies, shake hands in collusion over this deed (Luke 23:6-12; Acts 4:27). Once they were enemies, but after the crucifixion, they become friends.

Girard goes on to say that in Christianity, the ritual of eucharist in which bread and wine are given and which retells the story of the crucifixion of Jesus, reveals the "scapegoat mechanism," exposing this myth for what it truly is, a myth created to keep our society together. But has this fable actually been shown to be the wizard behind the curtain? In many Christian denominations and circles, the narrative continues to be reinforced by the idea that God requires a sacrifice in order for society to be healed. The scapegoat is not unmasked but is perpetuated in many of our churches.

Bob Ekblad, in a study of Isaiah, shows that in the Septuagint, the earliest translation of the Hebrew Scriptures into Greek, the translators were careful not to identify God as the source of the suffering of the figure known as the "suffering servant."[12] This passage of poetry from Isaiah describes a person who is stricken and punished, despite being innocent:

> Who would have believed what we just heard?
> When was the LORD's power revealed through him?
> He sprouted up like a twig before God,

like a root out of parched soil;
he had no stately form or majesty that might catch our attention,
no special appearance that we should want to follow him.
He was despised and rejected by people,
one who experienced pain and was acquainted with illness;
people hid their faces from him;
he was despised, and we considered him insignificant.
But he lifted up our illnesses,
he carried our pain;
even though we thought he was being punished,
attacked by God, and afflicted for something he had done.
He was wounded *because* of our rebellious deeds,
crushed *because* of our sins;
he endured punishment that made us well;
because of his wounds we have been healed.
All of us had wandered off like sheep;
each of us had strayed off on his own path,
but the LORD caused the sin of all of us to attack him.
(Isaiah 53:1-6 NET, emphasis mine)

In this translation, the writer(s) make it clear that it is *not* that the servant died *for* our sins, as a substitute that God chose to bear the punishment for our transgressions, but that the servant died *because* of the sins and rebellious deeds of others. In other words, sin caused the *han* inflicted on God's representative.

Psychologist and pastor Santo Calarco points out that in the context of the passage, we can see that the servant heals *because* of his wounds, despite what was done to him.[13] The problem with translation work is that every translation is an interpretation, and translators choose words that reflect what they are attempting to show their reader. What is curious about many English translations of Isaiah 53 is the use of the Hebrew preposition *me*, which can mean "from," "with," "for," or "because." See the examples of the word below that I've italicized:

- And *by* His scourging we are healed. (v. 5 NASB)
- *For* the transgression of my people, to whom the stroke was due? (v. 8 NASB)
- and *by* his wounds we are healed. (v. 5 NIV)
- *for* the transgression of my people he was punished. (v. 8 NIV)

If we say "by" in one case, why do we say "for" in the other case if the same word was used? If I say "*by* the transgression of my people he was punished," that changes the meaning drastically. Instead of saying that he was a substitute *for* the punishment of others, now it says that he was punished *because* of what others have done. This translation makes a world of difference.

In Christian history this passage has been applied to Jesus and specifically to Jesus' death on the cross. In 1 Peter, the writer interprets the Isaiah passage to show how Christ bore the sins of humanity in his body, and how through this, healing comes:

> For to this you have been called, because Christ also suffered for you, leaving you an example, so that you should follow in his steps.
> "He committed no sin,
>   and no deceit was found in his mouth."
> When he was abused, he did not return abuse; when he suffered, he did not threaten; but he entrusted himself to the one who judges justly. He himself bore our sins in his body on the cross, so that, free from sins, we might live for righteousness; by his wounds you have been healed. (1 Peter 2:21-24)

Calarco emphasizes, "Peter nowhere understands Isaiah 53 in the way it is preached nowadays in the Western church. When he quotes Isaiah 53, he says nothing about God putting sins onto Jesus in order to punish him on our behalf in order to satisfy his wrath!"

Calarco continues, "Jesus endured violence, didn't retaliate, but instead healed the crowds in spite of it by absorbing their violence!"[14]

The most important part of the poem is verse 10, which some Bibles translate as "Yet it was the will of the LORD to crush him with pain." Translators often include a footnote at the end of this line that says, "The meaning of Hebrew is uncertain," indicating that this is their best guess at the translation, but it is only an interpretation. The Septuagint reads:

> The LORD wishes to cleanse Him of His wound, and if you give an offering for sin . . .

In Ekblad's translation, it reads:

> And the LORD desires to purify him of the plague;
> If you would give a sin offering,
> Your soul will see a long-lived prosperity
> and the LORD desires to take away.[15]

This is quite a departure from the previous translation. God's will was *not* to crush the servant but to cleanse his wound, and by the healing of the servant, to heal all humanity.

We need not spend time on Greek and Hebrew passages of ancient texts to simply ask the question, Can punishment bring healing? If sin is the problem, and the solution to eradicating sin is punishment, does punishment actually destroy sin? Punishment might satisfy a tenet of the law, but God is not a set of rules. Numerous scholarly journals and books detail how punishment, whether "positive" or "negative," does not change behavior in the way that positive reinforcement does. But sociological and psychological research does not provide an answer to the broader theological question of whether God needs punishment, especially the forcefulness of violent punishment, to accomplish what God needs to do. This answer is easily found in the life of Jesus. It is also found in the book of Revelation, which is ironic, because the book contains a host of violent imagery.

LOVE CHANGES GOD

A helpful way in understanding how God can be changed by love and how this suffering God can be a model for healing is in a comparison of two images, one medieval and one contemporary. Augustine's model of God as lover, beloved, and love can also be seen in light of Jürgen Moltmann's image of the one who forsakes, the forsaken, and forsakenness.[16] All true love involves the risky possibility of being forsaken by the other. This is the forsakenness that God experienced at the cross. Thomas Aquinas, in his *Summa theologiae*, talks about how God gave Jesus up to the cruelty of humanity at the cross.[17] This was the risk that Jesus was willing to take in embodying humanity and living with us and loving us with unrestrained love.

God's love is the willingness of God to suffer and be changed in suffering. Both the Eastern and Western church fathers believed in God's changelessness, often called God's "impassibility." But as Moltmann notes, they did not rule out God's willingness to change.[18] God might not be able to suffer change as the result of outside influences, but why could not God allow God's own self to change—to actively change? God is not like a large, immoveable, adamant rock. God is someone who can and does become vulnerable to the aches and pains of love. If "God is love," then God is also willing to be vulnerable to pain and change. God is the possibility of forsakenness. Love, by nature, changes us, and if God is love, then God is open to the possibility of change. Consider this statement: "I'm willing to love, but I'm not willing to change." How ridiculous is that? Anyone who has the slightest experience with love knows that love requires us to change. This is why love is so terribly frightening.

When we are in a relationship, we grow in knowledge of each other. This knowledge adds to the love that we have for one another. This knowledge changes who we are, and who we are is often painfully revealed to us. One can say that God knows all and therefore is not subject to pain. But what if God's knowledge of us is not like that of a supercomputer that can calculate everything we might say and do? Instead, what if God's knowledge of us is based on our love of God and God's love for us? God is always making God's self open to us so that we might make ourselves open to God. Rather than merely a command to obey, God's love is an open invitation to dance.

If God knows all of who we are, then why does God need to love us, and why do we need to love God? A static God does not need to love or be loved. A personal God bares all to us. Jesus tells of God's gracious love in the story of the older son, younger son, and father, often called the story of the prodigal son (Luke 15:11-32).[19] My retelling is as follows:

Once upon a time there were two brothers. The younger, more spoiled one, asked for his inheritance to be given before his father died.

The father replied, "You can't legally do that. But if you want to leave my house, go!"

So the son left home penniless and found himself on the streets.

One day he thought, "Why am I sleeping here in the park when there is a nice memory foam mattress at my father's house? I can go home and be hired as one of his servants."

So he returned home and waited in his father's office.

His older brother, a really nice and handsome guy, walked into the room perplexed.

"Why did you return? You had all the freedom out there to be whatever you wanted, and to do whatever you wanted, and you came back to this place," said the older son.

"Well, freedom is not all that it was cut out to be . . ." the younger son replied.

Immediately, their father burst into the room and said, "I heard my son was back, and boy do I hope you learned your lesson."

"I've sinned before heaven and earth, Father," the younger son confessed.

"Yes, you did. Yes, you did. And your mother is worried sick about you. But here's what you must do to make it right."

Meanwhile, the older brother was nodding his head in agreement.

"First, someone has to be punished for these sins," the father said.

"Yes," agreed the older son.

The father continued, "Because I love you, my boy, I will make your brother pay the penalty for your crimes."

"What?" screamed the eldest son.

"Guards, take him now," the father instructed.

The guards bound the older son and dragged him out to be flogged and executed.

This is not the way that Jesus tells the story, but I recast it this way to drive home the point that Jesus did not preach the penal substitutionary view of atonement or original sin. His version of the story is about a returning son who thinks that he is beyond redemption and forgiveness. It is also a narrative that is directed toward the religious people of Jesus' day, and one that challenges their views about the openness and vulnerability of God.

Jesus' version of the story in Luke 15:11-32 begins with a son asking for his father's inheritance, to spend now, not after his father has died. This story is about those who do not understand the relationship that they presently have with God and the abundance of being in God's presence. The father gives the son everything; all that belongs to the father is his to receive. This is not a description of a wrathful and demanding God wanting children to obey an arbitrary "law," but of someone willing to provide everything, even when those receiving the provisions spend them frivolously. The father loves openly and gives all that he has, while the younger son spends his share of the inheritance on whatever he desires. Then a severe famine, a symbol of scarcity, ravages the land.[20] The son finds employment on a pig ranch, a scandalous job for a Jewish boy, and becomes so hungry that he is willing to eat pig food. This is when he comes to his senses. Why is he starving when there is plenty at home?

As the younger son returns home, the father sees his boy at a distance and runs to embrace him. The father was waiting this whole time, waiting and hoping that his son would return. The younger son believes that he is unworthy to be a son, unworthy even to be called a son, and confesses that he has "sinned against heaven and earth." But the father does not share this perspective. For the father, the son's return is like the return of someone lost who has been found, who was once dead, but is now alive.[21]

Just before this story, Jesus tells two other stories about being lost and being found, the parables of the lost sheep and the lost coin (Luke 15:1-10). Neither story portrays being lost as inherently bad, or sinful. In this parable, the father throws a lavish feast and tells the servants to clothe his boy. But the older son looks on in disapproval. Like many older siblings, myself included, he wonders why the youngest child is so spoiled. He is jealous at what the father has done for his brother and complains to his father, "You never threw me a party." The father pleads for the older son to join the celebration, saying, "You know all I have is yours." The religious people of Jesus' time did not understand the abundance that they had received from God. They did not comprehend the grace that was offered to them, and they lived as if they did not have access to the richness of God's mercy and love (Ephesians 2:4). This was why Jesus was a threat. He gave the people plentiful access to God, something that the religious people felt they had a right to monopolize. In their view, there was not enough God to go around.

If we continue to live within what is known as utilitarian ethics, where, as Mr. Spock says in *Star Trek*, "the good of the many outweighs the good of the one or the few," then we will all lose. The many will not understand the richness that those few can provide to improve the quality of life for everyone. Those who live according to extremely exclusionist and protectionist mentalities do not see how denying one immigrant entrance might deny the future of one doctor who would cure cancer, or of one great artist, or of one Nobel Peace Prize winner. They see immigrants as nothing more than a drain on the system. Many of us live as if we have a monopoly on God and, on this earth, on grace and resources. We are living at the expense of others. We are not willing to enter into the risky business of loving as God loves and embracing as God embraces.

Jesus' life of passive resistance does not mean he was passive or neutral about the sin and hurt in the world. Instead, he conquered sin and death through actively loving others and resisting the forces of evil. He did not return evil for evil, but confronted evil with powerful love, love that sought the best outcome for people. Seeking peace requires entering conflict, even creating the possibility of more conflict by virtue of one's presence. Peace requires that we do not give in to the oppressors' strategies and goals but rather transform them into opportunities for life-giving crises—Rosa Park's "nah," or Gandhi's hunger strikes. Sometimes seeking peace involves healing, and sometimes it requires confronting the power and privilege of political and religious elites. The story of the father, older son, and younger son demonstrates these relationship dynamics and illustrates that God's vulnerability is revealed to the world, not in wrath, but in embrace.

At the end of Le Guin's story about Omelas, some of the townspeople cannot face the bargain Omelas offers, so they choose to walk away. "They go on," Le Guin writes. "They leave Omelas, they walk ahead into the darkness, and they do not come back. The place they go toward is a place even less imaginable to most of us than the city of happiness. I cannot describe it at all. It is possible that it does not exist. But they seem to know where they are going, the ones who walk away from Omelas."[22]

But we do not have to live with binary choices, to either accept our situation or leave. We have a third choice: to create a world in which individuals and communities can receive healing. We can confront the evils before us. We do not have to live with broken systems. We do not have to return hurt for hurt, pain for pain. There is a third way, a third road.

How can the wounds of one man cleanse the wounds of humanity? We can only be healed when we look upon those wounds and see the sin and violence humans have perpetrated toward the other, and when we see that is the cause of their hurt. Those sins may not even be sins that we committed, but that were inflicted by another. But the trauma they created cannot be masked or glossed over, regardless of how difficult this may be. By the same token, we cannot wait until the offenders or perpetrators change their ways. Sometimes offenders are confronted, caught, brought to court, and punished. Sometimes they do not come to terms with what they are doing and remain unaware. More often than not, we will have the need to find healing even before the perpetrators of harm in our lives have come to terms with what they have done.

In the next chapter, we will look at how healing can take place in a world where the cycles of sin and *han* seem to be unceasing. How can the sting of death finally be defeated?

Enfleshment

The incarnation, the entering of God into the world in the form of a person. This challenges the mind/body, spiritual/material distinction that is found in ancient Gnosticism and modern Cartesian philosophy, which question the goodness of the body.

6

THE DEATH OF DEATH

Where, O death, is your victory? Where, O death, is your sting?

—1 CORINTHIANS 15:55

Darkness lasted only three days. But those days are an eternity to the one who had known only life.

During those days he is not absent from God, but only absent from those he loves. His body is buried in the tomb and a rock rolled over the mouth of the cave.

This is death—not the end of love, but the end of the reason for love. The laughter has ended. The meals with his friends are no more. His conversations with the women have ceased. What he can learn from them and what he can teach them are gone. They cannot grow old together. They cannot live life together.

Violence has taken all that away.

He had brought his friend Lazarus out from the clutches of death; others, too, he had brought back from the dead. For him, death holds no power. But to experience death firsthand is something else. To know firsthand what many fear and speculate upon, but has been foreign to him until he had to face it himself. He has become intimate with death, has kissed it, but has not embraced it.

This is not the end, but a passage from one life to the next life. It is how he has come to see his existence, with new eyes, with new everything. His body has been renewed, not replaced but transformed. His scars, the many scars that tattoo his body, are still there.

The wounds are healed, and he can continue to heal others. More than ever he understands what his mission is about.

From the dark he emerges.

———

I was called to a hospital emergency room. A four-year-old boy had been rushed in by the paramedics, and doctors and nurses were performing CPR on him. His small dark body lay on the white table, being moved around like a doll, while his parents waited just outside. They told me their son had started vomiting and then had a seizure. They immediately called 911 and an ambulance was dispatched. Now the couple was frantic.

A nurse asked me to come into the room and told me that there was nothing more they could do. The boy had contracted a case of meningitis that had gone undiagnosed and not been appropriately treated. Now his lifeless body lay on the emergency room table. All such news, especially when it comes in the middle of the night, seems like a dream to me, as if I were numb and outside of my own body.

We stepped outside the room to tell the parents. I could see the look of disbelief on the face of the boy's father. Then he announced,

"I'm taking my boy home." As he started to move toward the bed to grab his son, I jumped between them.

Hospital chaplains are trained to let family members grieve in their own way. We are taught that grief comes in many forms and that we should allow those who are grieving to do what they need to do. But this man could not take his dead son from the hospital. If he tried, there would be trouble between him and hospital security, and I did not want to see that happen.

The nurse did not know what to do. "No, please," she begged.

The father declared, "My boy is not dead. He's just sleeping."

I reached out to hold the father, who was my height, but probably twice my weight.

The boy's mother was in a corner weeping, deep in her own shock.

"I'm sorry," I said. "I'm sorry."

I reached out to embrace the father, and he held me tightly, weeping with loud groans, collapsing to the floor in tears, still holding on to me. Not by choice, I ended up down on the floor with him.

We rolled around on the ground, two grown men, in a mess of tears and wails. It felt biblical, like Jacob wrestling with God, trying to steal a blessing. This time, the face of God was dark-complexioned and African, and God was screaming because his son had just died. God had pinned a small Vietnamese man to the floor to show him that life is too short and often cruel, that parents lose their children to preventable diseases every day, and that we do not get any guarantees. I remember God's snotty nose and bloodshot eyes. They stared at me, asking why.

I did not have answers for God.

After a while, the dust settled, and we regained our composure. The boy's parents understood what had happened and that they needed to figure out their next steps. I left them alone with their boy.

Returning to the cold corridor, my soul was drained, and I needed to fill myself with coffee. My work as a chaplain was like this many days and nights.

THE BITTER TASTE OF DEATH

When I was a hospital and hospice chaplain, death was all too common. Death was a scent I could smell in the air, palpable. It was not a stench, like the smell at a nursing home, but a weight, a heaviness. Even after many years of being at the bedsides of dying people, presiding over funerals, and being with the friends and family of a deceased person, I still do not understand death. Philosophically, I do not comprehend the reason that we die. I understand the biology behind death, that the telomeres in our DNA eventually degrade over time. But there seems to be no *reason* that life should end. Biology should be on the side of life. I understand accidents and premature deaths, but not natural deaths. Death is such a recurring experience that we see it as a part of life, even though it need not necessarily be so. *Why* should we die?

The Eastern fathers believed that death came into the world through the first couple, Adam and Eve, as a consequence but not as a punishment. Adam and Eve, the representative humans, could have feasted on the tree of life and lived forever, but they chose to disobey God. As a result, they were expelled from the garden and an angel with a flaming sword was placed at its east side so that they could not return and eat from the tree of life (Genesis 3:24). This passage in the book of Genesis, and others like it, is an etiology, an explanation of why we have death in the world. It is not meant to be scientific, or even logical, but gives a reason because we need reasons in order to find meaning.

The Eastern fathers believed that death was passed down from Adam, from generation to generation, and that because of death we experience sin as a consequence. This explanation is very different from Augustine's view, which depicts the relationship as reversed—sin is inherited, and death is a result of sin as a punishment. For Augustine, we experience death because of sin. For the Western church, sin is the problem; for the Eastern church, death is the problem.

These fine distinctions may seem irrelevant to the average reader, but I want to point out that where one puts the emphasis determines how one tries to deal with the problem. For instance, if you tell your doctor, "My foot hurts," the doctor might say that the problem is with your foot and that the solution is amputation. However, the problem might actually be with your shoe. If bad shoes are the cause of your pain, the solution will be completely different.

For perpetrators, the real sinners, the diagnosis might actually be sin and the treatment, salvation. But salvation does not mean salvation from the fiery damnation of hell, but salvation from the system of evil and continued victimization of others. It is salvation from the perpetrators' own personal hell and from the perpetuation of sin that unfolds in their own lives. The wounded, however, need healing for the wounds that have resulted from the trauma of abuse, repair of damage from systems that demean and degrade, and liberation from victimization.

In chapter 3, I mentioned that sin is *not* the primary problem for God. Sin is a parasite that needs to be dealt with because it affects and infects others and the world in which we live, but treatment involves looking for the root cause. The larger problem, one that is more persistent and weightier, is death. Death is a reality that we face daily.

God faced death at the Roman cross and faced death each day that Jesus drew breath. Death pursued the infant Jesus. Death followed him throughout his ministry. Death sought to conquer him. The fear of death brings about a system of scarcity. Death brings finality and an end in a way that sin does not. Sin can lead to death, but as the apostle Paul says, "Death is the last enemy" (1 Corinthians 15:26 CEB). For the Eastern fathers, death is what led to sin.

There are two kinds of death that biblical authors such as Paul of Tarsus speak about: physical death and spiritual death. These two kinds of death are often conflated and confused by modern readers because the first-century authors did not see a dualism between the spiritual and the material in the way we do now. Our lives include both a final, physical end and, throughout our life, many "deaths," which may at times be caused by sin, whether the sin is committed by us or against us. These little defeats may come in the form of the loss of a job or the end of a relationship or other perceived failures. When Paul writes that "the wages of sin is death" (Romans 6:23), he is talking about a daily payment of death when one sins. It is these little deaths that remind us of our mortality.

In my own life, I have had many such experiences, including personal struggles and defeats, leaving jobs and careers, and mistakes and failures in relationships, in which I have lived as though dead, not unlike a zombie. The death that takes place at the end of our lives, whenever and however it occurs, is the last insulting blow. This finality reminds us that all our successes are merely vanishing dew. This death is the chief obsession of the writer of Ecclesiastes.

But much of our life, and especially life in the West, is motivated by fear of this physical death. The psychoanalyst Sigmund Freud is correct in diagnosing our motivations as grounded in sex and death. However, it is not only some innate drive toward pleasure that guides us, but the constant reminder that life has an absolute finality. All our projects, however big or small, will be put to rest. All our ambitions and goals, all our desires and dreams, all the things we hope and seek, have an eventual end.

For the ancient Greeks, and perhaps for many of us, the only potential for immortality is through procreation. However, our progeny are not guaranteed to achieve anything greater than we have done or sought to do. Some try to unfairly burden their children with dreams and ambitions that they themselves have not fulfilled. Some parents seek to make their children into the likeness and image of themselves in order to fulfill their dreams that have been dashed by life. These actions are driven by death.

Socrates claims that we fear death not because we fear what is unknown, but because we think we know something about death.[1] Socrates saw certainty as what kept people from entering into death in a dignified and respectful manner. His agnosticism about what death had in store helped him embrace it and drink the hemlock as his death sentence. In the West, most people seem to hold one of two ideas about existence in the afterlife: an annihilationist view, in which death brings an absolute finality to life, or an otherworldly existence in a place called "heaven." For many Western Christians, heaven is a place where only "believers" go after death, a place only for those who "accept Jesus as their Lord and Savior." Heaven promises a transcendent existence for some, possibly only for the relatives they love, and not for others, who will exist in "hell," the place of damnation, in the afterlife.[2] However, Jesus' teaching about this kind of existence is sparse and allegorical at best. Gehenna, the place of torment that Jesus speaks about, is based on a valley in Jerusalem where child sacrifices were made using fire (Jeremiah 7:31; 19:2-6). Gehenna is outside the city and is a metaphor for exclusion from the community. But this seems to be not the place where God condemns people, but the place where people find their own condemnation. Talk about "heaven" is indeed an "opiate of the masses." The empire (whether it's ancient Rome, or England, or the United States) likes citizens to concentrate on otherworldly existence because a focus on the kingdom/kin-dom challenges the existence of the current government.

Heavenly existence or annihilation need not be the only options for our understanding of the afterlife. Death can be seen as transitional and not exclusionary. In such a view, death is a door, a temporary end, a rest, not a full stop.

In one of Jesus' "I am" statements, which reflect the "being-ness" of God, Jesus says, "I am the resurrection and the life" (John 11:25). For Jesus, the resurrection is not so much an event at the end of time as it is a possibility. The Pharisees, as a result of the Jewish exile in Babylon (597–539 BCE), had adopted a view of the afterlife that included what was known as "the resurrection of the dead," a time when all bodies would rise and be judged by God. Before this belief developed, the Hebrew Scriptures only spoke about a shadow world, something they called *Sheol*, often translated "the pit" or "the grave." This was the destination for all people after death. Later, Sheol was incorporated into the Greek view of Hades. It was not until the early Middle Ages that the church developed doctrines of hell as a fiery place to which souls are condemned and where they are tormented, with varying interpretations by different theologians.[3] Jesus' audience, and especially those educated by the Pharisees, would have believed in the resurrection. When Jesus came to the tomb of his friend Lazarus, he told those present that Lazarus would rise again, and they replied that they believed this because they had been taught that all souls would someday be resurrected at the judgment. But Jesus was speaking about another kind of resurrection, a resurrection that we all can enter because Jesus is "the resurrection and the life." Jesuit priest Richard Rohr writes, "Salvation for me, and for many of the early Eastern Fathers of the Church, was not a question of *if*—but only a question of *when*—and *how* much you want it."[4] I would add that salvation for the Eastern fathers did not mean salvation from hell, but meant healing, wholeness, and flourishing.

Jesus embodied life, eternal life. The word *eternal* (Greek *aion*, the root of the English word *eon*) means forever, a description of quantity. But combined with the word *life* (Greek *zoe*), it conveys a quality of life that we experience now, in view of life in the resurrection to come. Some English translations use "abundant life" or "life to the full" to convey the meaning of eternal life. Eternal life is maximum life, extraordinary life, life to the brim. This life conquers both the death that is the end of the body and the little deaths that strike us throughout our lives, both physically and spiritually. Eternal life is not some eternal postmortem existence. Jesus embodied a "resurrected life," not life for some distant heavenly existence. This kind of life is ultimately enduring because it passes down a legacy that is eternal for all generations. We can find this way of living at the creative intersection where our story of *han* enters the story of another.

THE CREATIVE INTERSECTION OF *HAN* AND STORY

Many people subsist in the trash pits of Brazil; they are the *catadores*, the garbage pickers. They live in their own hell. The documentary *Waste Land* follows well-known artist Vik Muniz on his three-year project through the world's largest garbage dump, Jardim Gramacho. The landfill is located outside Rio de Janeiro and is where the catadores pick through trash to find things that they can either sell or recycle. As soon as the garbage trucks arrive and dump their waste, the catadores swarm in to gather what they can, like children on Christmas Day. But life is difficult for those who seek to live off what others have thrown away.

Muniz wanted to help the catadores to see the beauty in this trash and to collaborate with them to turn it into art. The people and trash become the subjects of art, as Muniz re-creates artist tableaux. Garbage becomes art and becomes transformative in the lives of people. Among the trash heaps, Muniz creates a place, a world, an alternative reality for the people of Rio de Janeiro. Muniz's own story is one of finding his own place in the world and creating with limited resources. He tells a story about returning to New York from Europe with about $100 to his name, a piece of Plasticine, a camera, and some film. Muniz made a sculpture with the Plasticine and took a picture of it. But because he only had one lump of Plasticine, he could only make one sculpture. So he destroyed what he had created, sculpted a new piece, and took a picture of it. He eventually took sixty images that became the art for his first solo show in 1992, which featured the photographs of his sculptures next to empty pedestals where the sculptures should have been.

The intersection of Muniz's life with the lives of the catadores flowered in this art. It is in this kind of relationship between one's own story and the story of another that we find beauty in life. This is the essence of what it means to live the fullest kind of life.

Lily Yeh, known as "the barefoot artist," says that "the broken places are my canvases."[5] Yeh immigrated with her mother from China, and her family story is one of struggle and brokenness. Her father, a general in the Chinese military during World War II, left his first wife and children for Yeh's mother. The shame of this betrayal followed Yeh's father, and then Yeh, throughout their lives. When her family immigrated to the United States, Yeh studied art in Philadelphia and later found herself in a dance school in North Philly. There she worked to help the community develop ways to beautify the city and spread arts education. For the next eighteen years, Yeh was the president of the Village of Arts and Humanities in North Central Philadelphia and went on to spread her work throughout the world in war-torn places such as Rwanda.

At times, people need more than words to reconcile with their past, and Yeh provides a language that transcends cultural barriers. In the documentary *The Barefoot Artist*, Yeh helps some of the survivors of the Rwandan genocide create a monument to both the survivors and the victims of the genocide. She observed that the mass graves where bones were piled and buried were often marked only by concrete structures, or sometimes by a concrete slab. "There was no poetry; there was no beauty," she says. "To truly honor the dead we have to bring beauty and honor them in that light." The Rwanda Healing Project was created as a collaboration with those survivors to help bring closure to wounds that can still be palpably felt.

Yeh's own healing came after her father's death, when she tried to reunite with the family that her father had left when he married her mother. In this way, the guilt of Yeh's father and the shame that Yeh experienced could be put to rest, and Yeh's wounds were stitched closed through the tears and forgiveness of her father's previous family. Often, the intersection of our lives with the lives of others is a way in which we work out the deep wounds and hurts in our lives, the places of shame. Both Muniz and Yeh found healthy and constructive ways to address their suffering, ways that brought hope and healing to themselves and to others.

TOUCHING THE WOUNDS OF *HAN*

"But those who drink of the water that I will give them will never be thirsty. The water that I will give will become in them a spring of water gushing up to eternal life," Jesus says to the Samaritan woman at the well (John 4:14). She had been disgraced and shunned. In their culture, not only did women and men refrain from socializing in public in this way, but Jews and Samaritans also did not interact like this. Even Jesus' disciples question his actions (v. 27). Samaritans were descendants of the people of Canaan who had intermixed with Jews. They worshiped in the same ways as Jews, with the exception that they worshiped in the places that the Jews had abandoned as worship sites when Solomon's temple in Jerusalem became the central place of Jewish worship.

Because the life of the Samaritan woman has been one of either constant loss or disgrace or rejection, there is much emptiness that needs to be filled. Contrary to many common interpretations today, she has not done anything wrong or immoral, but is shamed by her community for living with someone who is not her husband.[6] Jesus' awareness of her situation is not so much one of indignation, but simply one of acknowledgment of her situation. Jesus does what others could not do—he sits with her and is with her in her pain. He sees her shame and offers her something more, in the form of a relationship with a source of life that will overflow into the lives of others. Both the woman and Jesus cross cultural boundaries, gender and ethnic lines. Jesus asks her—begs her—for water, and he offers her living water.[7] The exchange is mutual; each learns something from the other. Jesus learns about the losses in her life, and she learns about him as the Messiah who shares how to worship "in spirit and truth" (v. 24). He does not simply offer her belief *about* him, but offers an opportunity to establish deep trust in a source of life that can bring forth something eternal.

Woundedness gives us choices. At the crossroads of *han* is an important, life-changing choice to take either the road toward further bitterness and resentment, which leads eventually to violence and death, or the road of creativity and renewal that leads to life. Calvin believed that the wounds that witnesses saw on the body of the resurrected Jesus were temporary. "Do not place faith in the wounds. They do not reveal truth," he wrote, pointing to Thomas, the doubter, and exhorting, "Wake up slumbering disciples." Theologian Shelly Rambo notes that for Calvin, those who doubt Jesus' resurrection and must put their finger into his wounds before believing are "lazy" disciples. Thomas needed to be "violently drawn back to faith by sensual means."[8] For Calvin, the wounds of Jesus are for those "weak in faith," and it is not through touching and seeing that the believer comes to faith, but through hearing and believing. Calvin found it difficult to believe that Jesus' wounds could be an eternal part of his body and argues that the ultimate "glorification" of Jesus will erase these wounds. In his commentary on John 20:20, Calvin wrote, "But if any person should infer from this [Christ's revealing his wounds], that Christ has still the wounded side and the pierced hands, that would be absurd; for it is certain that the use of the wounds was temporary, until the Apostles were fully convinced that he was risen from the dead."[9]

Calvin's predecessor Martin Luther held a similar view. But prior to Calvin and Luther, the early church fathers, up through the time of Aquinas, acknowledged that Christ retains these wounds.[10] Christ's wounds portray a connection between God's involvement in creation and how God relates eternally.[11] God's wounds show God's vulnerability to receiving *han*, and also the continual nature of God as one of love and vulnerability to abandonment. Just as life, true life, exists in the tension between wounds and healing, and between love and abandonment, Jesus retains his scars, and we are invited to touch and see them. When we touch the wounds of the risen Christ, we are given the ability to touch our own scars and to know the possibility of life for the *han*-ridden. Those who have suffered from the perpetrators of *han* will be healed. Death is not the end, and life can spring forth.

The Japanese art technique of *kintsugi* involves repairing broken dishes or pottery with a mixture of lacquer and gold, silver, or platinum. The philosophy of this art is to embrace brokenness and see beauty in it. *Kintsugi*, meaning "golden seams," is also related to the Japanese aesthetic of imperfection called *wabi-sabi* (roughly translated as "irregularly-aged"). The first time I saw the technique of *kintsugi* applied, a Japanese-Hawaiian potter created a beautiful ceramic piece, but after he had finished shaping it on the wheel, he deliberately broke a piece off, marring it with his clay-carving knife. For those of us with a Western view of beauty as perfectionism, this type of artistry might make our obsessive-compulsive tendencies go berserk. Is this why the West has difficulty with a God who is open to being broken and scarred, a God who is vulnerable and who allows God's own being to be vulnerable to hurt? Western views of purity and perfection might drive these ideas of immutability, but only the battered and broken God of the eucharist can feed and heal all.

When we are isolated and alone, it is difficult to touch and see these wounds, but within communities of healing we can receive these reminders and testimonies. These are communities not only of the wounded, but also of healers who wish to love, accept, and form covenants with the wounded. A delicate balance is required in order to create a space where those who have been wounded are able to live and thrive in spaces that might bring back reminders of hurt, as well as to find healing and wholeness. I've seen many churches where, because of poor leadership and skills, woundedness perpetuates more woundedness. Broken people often attract others like them, and physicians to the broken can easily become perpetrators of more damage if their own wounds have not been sufficiently treated. Many seminaries require statements of well-being from their applicants, but this does not go far enough. Like all counseling professions, seminarians should also be required to receive therapy and training in pastoral care. In some congregations, people put on their best faces and avoid showing vulnerability, even though many are deeply hurt. At other times, churches become safe havens and gathering spots for perpetrators of wounds. Many people, especially those in upper-middle-class and wealthy churches, imagine themselves in the role of the Hebrew slaves in Egypt, when in reality they are actually more like Pharaoh. However, the divide between those who cause hurt and those who suffer hurt is not that simple.

A woman once shared during a church service about a trauma she suffered in college, and how her church community had helped her to recognize the depth of her pain, but also to see the woundedness of her perpetrator. "I thought of what kind of brokenness a person must have in order to do that to someone," she said. This was a very generous act of forgiveness that neither I nor anyone else could have imposed on her. Only she could come to that conclusion, and she came to it by way of the love of her community. We are all wounded in some way, and we can all hurt others. Recognizing this does not and cannot mitigate the responsibility of those who intentionally cause harm and prey on others. Those who are the oppressors and perpetrators in our society need to change their attitudes and actions toward others. Only in realizing that they are also damaging themselves will they be able to cease the damage they are inflicting on others.[12]

Artist Andy Goldsworthy works with and in nature. His medium is tree branches, leaves, rocks, rain, rivers, and snow. Toward the end of the documentary *Leaning into the Wind*, Goldsworthy is working on an art piece with his daughter Holly. They are at the banks of a stream and Goldsworthy is covering his left hand in red flower petals. He talks about having done this piece before but says that this time he is assisted by his daughter, who covers his right, dominant hand with the petals. He describes the red petals as "bandages," as if Holly were dressing his wounds. He talks about the difficulty of letting someone else complete his work because he does not do well at delegating tasks, but he admits that she is more competent at the job than he is because she has a "delicate touch." After his daughter is finished, Goldsworthy steps into the stream. Slowly he dips both hands into the stream, and as the water pulls the petals away, his hands appear to be washed. The bloodied bandages fall away and become flower petals that float away.

The layers of imagery in this piece of art struck me as I watched— the help that is needed in bandaging another's wound, the patience and intimacy between two people who care about each other, the trust in the stream to complete the work, the healing that takes place in relationship to others and nature. How can we create communities that bring wholeness and healing to the world? In the final chapter of this book, I will talk about forms of justice, the work of reconciliation, *dan* (an alternative response to *han*), and calls to action that need to take place if we are to grasp at something more than wishful thinking and empty hopes.

DEATH, SIN, AND *HAN*

Death, sin, and *han* are interwoven into an intricate tapestry that makes up the air we all breathe. It is clear that God, as well as God's creation, is on the side of life. Sin occurs when we give in to the pull of death, to all that seeks to destroy life. As sociologist and educator Parker Palmer observes, we engage in practices that are either "death-dealing" or "life-giving."[13] We live within the creative tension of these two polarities. Death-dealing choices become quick fixes in a culture characterized by addiction, obsession with celebrity and power, and an attraction toward destruction rather than creation. Yet within death-dealing options, there is a semblance of life. In some ways, it is easier to tear down than to build up. At least tearing down gives us some purpose. This is the Nietzschean option, to seek meaning in violence toward others and the self.

Sin propagates in this cycle; where suffering, longing, and desire are not transformed, destruction multiplies and spirals down toward death. We know this from observing the consequences—a trail of destruction, lost relationships, hurt, and responsibility borne by those who did not cause the harm, the loneliness and isolation that we encounter at the end of each day. I've known too many leaders, seemingly successful professionals, who live this kind of existence. Among them are clergy, lawyers, doctors, engineers, teachers, and others who have all become accomplished in the act of "doing," but not in the art of "being." Neither "human" nor "being" is part of their agenda. But our vocations, our callings, are much higher than merely to work, earn money, and exist.

Building up requires that we creatively do something with life, a life that involves difficulty, pain, and suffering, but also joy and hope. Death is neither the final victor nor the last word. Within all of us is the "light [that] shines in the darkness" (John 1:5), and this light is ignited by the possibility of moving into the space of creative suffering. When we examine the *han* in our own lives and find healing for ourselves and others, we find the canvas for a life of meaning and creativity. For those who have sinned against others, this is also the intersection where we find repentance and new ways forward.

Jesus was always helping people turn from death to life. Death is most often the looming experience of something we cannot do anything about, the final mark of our mortality and finiteness, our utter dependency and vulnerability. If we take the Eastern fathers' view that sin is the result of our passions, our feelings in reaction to death, then we can see that much of our destructive behavior is a response to death. We feel helpless about death, and we act out of this fear of impending death, a fear that is intimately related to a sense of scarcity—the perception that life is limited. We sense that there is not enough time to do all that we want to do, nor enough resources. Control, power over others, attention seeking, and all sorts of malicious acts toward others and self center on these death-dealing decisions.

For both the sinner and the sinned-against, Jesus offers liberation from our fixation on dispelling the assaults and insults of death from our lives. For sinners, Christ offers freedom to love, and therefore to be loved. For the sinned-against, he offers empowerment to choose to confront, forgive, receive vocation, celebrate blessing, grieve, create peace, and engage in all sorts of life-giving acts. The Spirit offers the sinned-against the way of *dan*, a Korean term that means "to cut off." This is a strategy to prevent further hurt and end the cycle of sin. As a victim to the Roman cross, a rabbi shunned by his own religious tradition, a man constantly questioned about his pedigree—the son of a day-laboring carpenter, Jesus provides a way to live boldly in the world with authority and wholeness of being.

Figure 1. The creative intersection of han

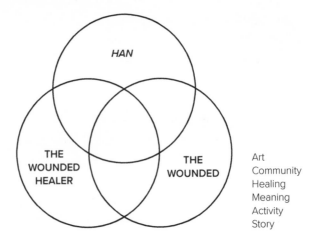

A picture of my uncle, my father's younger brother, hangs on a wall in my parent's home as a part of a makeshift altar. His black-and-white picture is almost a mirror of my appearance. During my late twenties, I looked almost exactly like him. Not many years after that picture was taken, his life was ended by the war. My uncle was serving in the South Vietnamese Army when his boat hit a mine. He was instantly killed. Each time I see that picture, I wonder what kind of life he would have had if war had not taken his life, whether he would have had a family and children. Then I reflect on my life and wonder how much of it I have wasted and whether I am making the most of what has been given to me, is given to me in each day, each breath.

Growing up in the United States, every move from state to state and town to town seemed like another ending of my life. Each move meant the end of friendships, the end of love. These experiences of loss and grief are sown deeply into my soul. They brought feelings of abandonment, eternal abandonment, God-abandonment, over and over again. My grief was the grief of the little Asian boy who met and played with a white girl in kindergarten and then, several weeks later, had to leave the school because his parents had to move to find work. The little boy left his first childhood love. The life I lived as a child is the migratory life of people whose lives were torn apart by war, people who have to piece themselves back together again and again.

When every departure and every change in relationship smells of death, why risk the pain of venturing into new experiences and journeys? Experience has made me wary, but also hopeful. I am deeply aware of both the impermanence of life and the strength of life, new life, renewed life. Life is insistent in overcoming death. This insistence has been built into nature, and also into the way God is at work within the world, within us and through us.

At a poetry reading, my good friend D. F. Brown recalled the trauma of the Vietnam War as an American vet. In "Bình Định Blues," Brown recites lyrics about a particular area, memories of which return again, and again: "bobbing in the waves off Qui Nhơn / central coast of always always."[14]

After the reading I told him that I was born in Qui Nhơn during the time he was stationed in Bình Định Province.

"I'm glad you made it here, my friend," Brown told me. "I'm glad we both made it here."

We shook hands and embraced.

Catadores

The name for garbage pickers in Brazil. Those who make their subsistence by picking through trash. This has become an occupation not only in South America, but also in Africa and Asia. The latter is the destination for much of the garbage (hundreds of millions of tons) that is shipped from the United States to be recycled. Even though the trash provides the benefit of wages, harm comes in the form of child labor and occupational health risks.

7

THE BIRTH OF KINGDOM

For Christians, the way to make the Holy Spirit truly present in the church is to practice thoroughly what Jesus lived and taught. It is not only true that Christians need Jesus, but Jesus needs Christians also for His energy to continue in this world.

—THÍCH NHẤT HẠNH, *Living Buddha, Living Christ*

Scared and anxious, the disciples wait in the upper room where they were often taught by their master. They cautiously anticipate the promise of the Spirit that will change all their lives. They are subdued by the fear that the women and men present there will not bring the message beyond these walls. Their *thầy*, their teacher, was a person who could cast out demons, heal the sick, feed the many, raise the dead, and without him they are aimless and without direction or purpose. Some of them have denied the master. Some of them ran away when the soldiers came for them. Nearly all, except the women, abandoned him at the cross. Now they have come to trust the testimonies of these women, but many are still apprehensive about what might come next.

When he finally visits them, he teaches them about the kingdom. They wonder when this kingdom will come, and he tells them that is not their concern, but he will empower them. They are to continue the work he started. Together they can do more than he could do alone. They will be his hands and feet to build the kingdom that is right before them, and also yet to come, the kingdom that is inside them and also manifesting through them.

They are to move forward, uncertain and scared, into the world. This is a world that will also persecute them. But their names will be remembered. They will pass down a legacy, perhaps to a few, but their work will continue through the women and men they inspire.

With them, he has birthed something new. He will continue to be with them, to walk with them, to go where this gospel might take them, to suffer and die, and be reborn again.

ALTERNATIVE HISTORIES

The 1915 silent movie *The Birth of a Nation* has received widespread criticism because of its attempt to rewrite history in order to muster sympathy for the South and credit the Ku Klux Klan for the reconstruction of post–Civil War America.[1] It portrays Lincoln and the Union as provocateurs of the war, Black men as sexually aggressive and violent, and American reconstruction in the South as a failure. The film's message is disturbing but is also a telling indicator of what some believe to be at the heart of reconciliation, peace, and unification for white Americans. *The Birth of a Nation* offers a vision of unification for the United States through the scapegoating of Black people, justifying even further violence and discrimination.

Regrettably, D. W. Griffith's film, which uses striking imagery and cinematic elements, is both a work of genius and a work of bigotry. The movie ends with a scene in which Black Union soldiers storm the house of Southern white families. Klansmen soldiers on horseback rush in to save the day. The movie concludes as the Northern Stoneman family and the Southern Cameron family host a double wedding: the daughter and son of the Stoneman family marry the son and daughter of the Camerons. Before the last title, these words appear on the screen: "Dare we dream of a golden day when the bestial War shall rule no more. But instead—the gentle Prince in the Hall of Brotherly Love in the City of Peace."

These words are followed by two striking images. One is a tableau of a warrior on horseback waving a sword and looming over a mass of people. On one side are piles of the dead, and on the other, those who are living but seemingly under a looming threat. The second picture is a figure of Jesus Christ (appearing, of course, as a white man). This is the image of peace.

The final title card reads: "Liberty and union, one and inseparable, now and forever." A superficial interpretation of these words and images would indicate that there is a way of war and a way of peace, and the one of peace is through Jesus Christ, ending the movie on a curious religious point. However, if we view the movie's end in light of the total narrative, we see that the peace described is a peace won at the expense of Black people in the United States. Reconciliation comes when the two white families marry, not when the nation confronts its violent history. In the film, the peace that is under Jesus Christ is one that excludes Black people, because they are not depicted as living in the same paradise as the Jesus image. The last image of Black people is one in which they are violent, surrendering their weapons, and being prevented from voting.

This work of racist propaganda was rightly criticized by the NAACP and other groups for its racist depictions and actors in blackface. But the true success of this film is not in its racist propaganda, but in the way it criminalizes itself. *The Birth of a Nation* reveals that racism was indeed a part of the genesis of the United States of America and shows us how this nation continues to scapegoat Black people and other people of color so that a relative "peace" can be achieved. The film reflects not only the filmmaker's views, but also a glimpse into this nation's inception and the continued efforts to either cover up these wounds of history or rewrite this history. Even so, the wounds still undeniably fester underneath the surface.

In 2016, actor and filmmaker Nate Parker reclaimed the title of the Griffith film to tell the story of Nat Turner, the leader of the 1831 rebellion by enslaved people. In an interview, Parker clarifies:

> When I endeavored to make this film, I did so with the specific intent of exploring America through the context of identity. So much of the racial injustices we endure today in America are symptomatic of a greater sickness—one we have been systematically conditioned to ignore. From sanitized truths about our forefathers to miseducation regarding this country's dark days of slavery, we have refused to honestly confront the many afflictions of our past. This disease of denial has served as a massive stumbling block on our way to healing from those wounds.[2]

I've repurposed the film title once again and reclaimed it for this chapter as a tool to challenge racism and white supremacy in America, to inspire a riotous disposition toward any and all injustices in this country (and abroad), and to promote honest confrontation in hopes that it will galvanize our society toward healing and sustained systemic change.

The fiction of the film became a myth, and therefore reality, for those white Americans who sought to form a united country through whiteness and white supremacy. This false narrative of peace continues until this day: We hear it in the lament that if only Americans were of one culture, one tradition, then America could be great again, and would again enjoy economic security and success. Even Black people would be employed—both in the film and in our history, masses of Black people are in the cotton fields, and they are all working.

REALITY AND WISHFUL THINKING

At some point in reading the Gospels with my students, the subject of the results of Jesus' sacrifice on the cross comes up. I often ask, "If Jesus' death took care of death, and therefore evil and sin, then why do we still struggle with widespread violence, war, racism, and hatred in the world?" This is a pressing question that many theologians answer with an unsatisfying "already/not yet" response. Are we simply to proclaim that Jesus eradicated things, even when we can see that they have not yet been dealt with, and then wait to see if this was really the case? That is a lot to ask, especially if one is the victim of these injustices. For those who do not live with hardships, who have access to resources and medical care, who do not worry about food and rent being paid each month, waiting for some sort of afterlife vindication is a possibility. But for those who don't have these luxuries and are the targets of daily oppression, the "not yet" is too far away.

RECONCILIATION: PIECING TOGETHER OUR BROKEN SELVES

Several terms that are often used in Christian and secular culture need to be defined and reimagined in order to move our country and our world toward healing and wholeness. In the following sections, I will respond to common questions and explore ways in which communities can come to reimagine, envision, and embody a new way of God's presence in the world.

One common argument against attempts at reconciliation questions the etymology of the word itself. "Reconciliation cannot happen, because we have not even 'conciled,'" the objection goes. In other words, how can reconciliation happen when we were not even friends in the first place? The Latin-based word *reconciliare* means "to bring back together" (from the Latin *conciliare*: to bring together), and it is rather troublesome to imagine that reconciliation could begin without an attempt at friendship.

But the language that Paul of Tarsus uses for reconciliation in Scripture focuses not on the difficulty of repairing friendships that have yet to be formed, but on the reality of the nature of persons. Paul's concern was ontological—about our essential nature—and not about the relational nature of reconciliation, odd as this may sound. He writes to the Corinthian congregations:

> From now on, therefore, we regard no one from a human point of view; even though we once knew Christ from a human point of view, we know him no longer in that way. So if anyone is in Christ, there is a new creation: everything old has passed away; see, everything has become new! All this is from God, who reconciled us to himself through Christ, and has given us the ministry of reconciliation; that is, in Christ God was reconciling the world to himself, not counting their trespasses against them, and entrusting the message of reconciliation to us. So we are ambassadors for Christ, since God is making his appeal through us; we entreat you on behalf of Christ, be reconciled to God. For our sake he made him to be sin who knew no sin, so that in him we might become the righteousness of God. (2 Corinthians 5:16-21)

Paul's understanding was that the narratives of Christ and of humanity merged within the events of the crucifixion and resurrection, and that these events tell of the essential oneness of God and humanity. The life of humans cannot be extricated from the life of God, as is seen in the life of Jesus, the Christ. This vision of a new creation is the vision for the restoration of what once was. All things were in God, and all things are now "in Christ." This being "in Christ" provides the possibility of reconciliation, but it is *like* a return to a former state where humans were one with God, and as a consequence, one with each other. I say that it is *like* the old state because in Christ's reconciliation all creation is not returned to an earlier state but rather is made new. Humans are no longer enemies with God, with others, and with their essential natures, but now are in a renovated, Christlike relationship, one that mirrors Christ's life.

Much of the criticism of the term *reconciliation* stems from Christians doing too little to work through issues of injustice, as well as focusing too much on how God and humans can once again be friends. In the above passage, Jesus appears to be doing the hard work of reconciling the world to God. The implication is that acts of sin and rebellion and feelings of guilt and shame have caused God to shun humanity. Following this line of thinking, it was Jesus' work in his death on the cross that turned God's face toward humans. This interpretation could not be further from the truth. God's work in Christ was always the work of "not counting their trespasses [or sins] against them" (v. 19). God was never angry with humans; it was the other way around.

If this is the case, then what part do humans play in this reconciliation? God's work of removing the animosity of humans might not seem to be enough to right the wrongs in this world, heal injustices caused by perpetrators of hurt and violence, and confront systemic evils. When humans do nothing to work at sowing peace in this world, then the reconciliation work of God cannot be accomplished. Justice work must be at the center.

JUSTICE: THE DIFFERENCE BETWEEN FAIR AND RIGHT

In the history of Western philosophy, the subject of justice is at the center of some of the most important philosophical works. The question "What is justice?" is at the center of Plato's *Republic*.

The voice of Socrates explores this very issue in his dramatic dialogues. *The Republic* is the Latin title of Plato's work and seems to describe a type of government, but the title in the original Greek is *Politeia*, or *The Politics*.[3] "Politics" deals with the communal good and the just management of resources for the common good. In Greek, the word *justice* is *dikaios*, and *just* is *dikaiosýnē*.[4] In the New Testament, this same Greek word for "just" is more often translated as "righteousness," which connotes a certain moral piety. But an upstanding citizen and a just person are not necessarily the same.

More often than not, when readers of the New Testament interpret Paul's citation of Hosea in Romans 1:17, "For in it the righteousness of God is revealed through faith for faith; as it is written, 'The one who is righteous will live by faith,'" they take it to mean that God is the only one who is right and that doing right can only come through faith in God. But what if we read the verse in terms of justice: "For in [the gospel] the justice of God is revealed through [God's] faithfulness for faith; as it is written, 'The one who is just will live by faith.'"

At the heart of the gospel is justice. What does the gospel, or "good news," look like? Because justice is part and parcel of the good news, the answer to that question must be governed by justice.

This good news does not simply mean that passive righteousness is given to believers. If God's work is to make all things right in the world, then this must mean that for believers, right actions, right thoughts, right virtues, right feelings, and right aesthetics are involved. It means that faith requires a contribution to the entire economy of the universe and is not only a matter of believing in something. Reformer Martin Luther believed in a righteousness that is given, declared, to Christians, because he believed that Christians cannot earn their own righteousness from God. This "forensic" righteousness was imputed by a righteous judge onto those who believe and confess. However, there is a large gulf between being declared righteous and living rightly. This is the difference between saying that we are free and living as if we are free (one can have all sorts of bondages). In other words, if we trust that God is doing right and acting justly in the world, then we are also required to do right and act justly (Micah 6:8).

The philosopher of the otherworldly "forms," Socrates was deeply interested in what justice is and how it plays out in this world of "shadows." Christians are called to be deeply invested in justice. If Christians believe that systems have become misaligned, that there is evil in the world, then there needs to be a way to join God's work in diligently doing the work of justice. When a person shoots up a school, killing innocent students and teachers, we cannot just call it an evil act and do nothing to change the culture of gun violence in our nation. "Thoughts and prayers" alone are excuses for keeping the status quo, for continuing the cycle of evil rather than preventing it. For those who perpetuate injustice and turn their faces away from those who suffer from it, God's kingdom will bring the toppling of their fortunes. For those who suffer injustice, God is a co-conspirator, helping to move the arc of history toward justice. Joining God in achieving this justice is a long and arduous work, helped by that for which the cosmos longs.

Minister and civil rights activist John Perkins describes reconciliation in terms of justice: "Justice is any act of reconciliation that restores any part of God's creation back to its original intent, purpose or image. When I think about justice that way, it doesn't surprise me at all that God loves it. It includes both the acts of social justice and the restorative justice found on the cross."[5]

Justice and reconciliation are tightly woven realities that fall apart if separated. Because our human nature—the way we function to achieve our purpose as human beings—is linked to justice, both justice and the work of restoring humanity offer ways forward in which healing can occur. Regrettably, some evangelical Christian

leaders, such as John MacArthur, have criticized the belief that social justice is a core part of Christianity.[6] MacArthur says that the
church's involvement in the social justice movement is concerning
because "the values borrowed from secular culture are currently un-
dermining Scripture in the areas of race and ethnicity, manhood and
womanhood, and human sexuality."[7] Leaders such as MacArthur
exalt private and individual relationships with God over social and
societal change. This attitude is consistent with Western culture and
attitudes that value individuality over collectivity and is a form of
cultural appropriation. These leaders are claiming that there is only
one way to do Christianity—from a Western, atomized lens.

In the Hebrew Scriptures and the New Testament, the prophets and apostles do not differentiate between social justice and any
other form of justice. Justice, if it is true justice, necessarily exhib-
its a social dimension—otherwise, where else can it be applied?
Consider Scriptures that deal with the treatment of those in need:

> Hear this, you rulers of the house of Jacob
>   and chiefs of the house of Israel,
> who abhor justice
>   and pervert all equity. (Micah 3:9)

> Thus says the LORD:
> For three transgressions of Israel,
>   and for four, I will not revoke the punishment;
> because they sell the righteous for silver,
>   and the needy for a pair of sandals—
> they who trample the head of the poor into the dust of the earth,
>   and push the afflicted out of the way;
> father and son go in to the same girl,
>   so that my holy name is profaned. (Amos 2:6-7)

> But let justice roll down like waters,
>   and righteousness like an ever-flowing stream. (Amos 5:24)

And in the New Testament:

Woe to you, scribes and Pharisees, hypocrites! For you tithe mint, dill, and cummin, and have neglected the weightier matters of the law: justice and mercy and faith. It is these you ought to have practiced without neglecting the others. (Matthew 23:23)

What good is it, my brothers and sisters, if you say you have faith but do not have works? Can faith save you? If a brother or sister is naked and lacks daily food, and one of you says to them, "Go in peace; keep warm and eat your fill," and yet you do not supply their bodily needs, what is the good of that? So faith by itself, if it has no works, is dead. (James 2:14-17)

Justice cannot be extricated from the gospel or from Christianity. The good news must be the news that God is doing something to right the wrongs of the world. God's justice is more often applied to people and society than to keeping a narrowly interpreted law. This is not to say that law is not unimportant to justice, but that the whole point of justice affects the way in which the law is applied.

In place of the word *righteousness*, perhaps we should use the word *rightness* to remind ourselves that justice is not only fairness, but also involves doing what is right. Children have a technique for fairly sharing something: "You split, and I pick." When children use this method of dividing up their goods, they are attempting to get at what is fair. Fairness is not just a relative notion, something that is arbitrary and abstract. We all want fairness. Imagine if in the act of splitting cookies or other treats, one child always gets to both split and pick. Then one day the rules change, and the child who has not had an opportunity to divide or choose now receives that opportunity. The rules are now fair, but is it right that there was such a long history in which this child did not receive the opportunity? In such a situation, rightness means something other than returning to rules that are equitable in the present. To have a truly just society, something must be changed, not only in the rules of the game, but in how different players should be treated on the basis of their history.

RETRIBUTIVE JUSTICE: AN EYE FOR AN EYE, WRONGLY INTERPRETED

Retributive justice is about repaying hurt with hurt; it is about getting even. The idea behind the standard of "an eye for an eye" is not to promote retributive justice, but to limit it. These limits specified that if an eye was injured, one could take only an eye as retribution, and not an entire life. By Jesus' day, this biblical allowance was taken as a command and deemed to be the standard of justice. However, Jesus understood that this form of justice could not end the cycle of violence. "An eye for an eye" justice continues the cycle of hurt and retribution. This retributive form of justice involves families, communities, and even entire countries in seeking retribution against one another, with the cycle continuing until no one is left standing. One example of the destructive potential of retributive justice can be seen in the conflict between Israel and Palestine over a piece of land roughly the size of New Jersey.[8] This conflict will only end if one side first decides that life is more than blood and land.

Theologian Miroslav Volf writes that Jesus "broke the vicious cycle of violence by absorbing it, taking it upon himself."[9] Volf knows firsthand the pain that resulted from the war between Croatia and Serbia, a conflict between Muslims and Christians in which retributive justice led to the death of many people he knew. This experience was the underlying impetus for Volf's award-winning book *Exclusion and Embrace*, in which he describes the radical embrace of God, who seeks to restore the world to God's self. God is not out for vengeance, Volf argues, even though God has declared that "vengeance is mine" (Deuteronomy 32:35). Vengeance cannot achieve the restoration and renewal of creation. It can only offer emotional satisfaction to victims by returning harm to those who have perpetrated harm, a temporary relief that is shallow compared to eternal restoration.

The book of Revelation, often misinterpreted because of its violent imagery, uses the image of a rainbow to link the narration to the story of the flood told in Genesis. In Genesis, the flood story demonstrates God's abhorrence of violence and shows that attempting to resolve violence through violence cannot be successful:

> The LORD saw that the wickedness of humankind was great in the earth, and that every inclination of the thoughts of their hearts was only evil continually. And the LORD was sorry that he had made humankind on the earth, and it grieved him to his heart. (Genesis 6:5-6)

The writers of Genesis record the story of God sending a flood but sparing Noah, his family, and the creatures on the ark. After the flood destroys all other life on earth, God provides a rainbow in the sky as a sign for Noah, a symbol of God's covenant promise to never again destroy the earth in this way (Genesis 9:12-15). Taken literally, this promise might seem false, given the continued natural disasters that have occurred throughout history, including the many floods in my state of Texas. But taken figuratively, this story tells of God's commitment to not use violence for violence. The solution to human violence was not the further destruction of life, but the provision of grace through the saving of life. In God's economy, all life is sacred:

> Only, you shall not eat flesh with its life, that is, its blood. For your own lifeblood I will surely require a reckoning: from every animal I will require it and from human beings, each one for the blood of another, I will require a reckoning for human life.

Whoever sheds the blood of a human,
    by a human shall that person's blood be shed;
for in his own image
    God made humankind. (Genesis 9:4-6)

Taking the life of another was condemned because the "image of God" is imprinted in all humans. To violate this image is to violate God. In the book of Revelation, the rainbow image is used as a reminder that violence is not the way of Jesus. John writes:

At once I was in the spirit, and there in heaven stood a throne, with one seated on the throne! And the one seated there looks like jasper and carnelian, and around the throne is a rainbow that looks like an emerald. (Revelation 4:2-3)

The image of Jesus sitting on a throne encircled by a rainbow is a picture of nonviolent covenant. The book of Revelation depicts the triumph of Jesus over violence. The image of the Lion/Lamb as one standing, but who was slain, gives witness to Jesus as the victim of violence (Revelation 5:6). Jesus is depicted as a lion, the symbol of King David's reign, but this ruler is one who gives life rather than takes it. Although Jesus was violently executed, through the power of the resurrection he stands. The cross was a consequence of the life he lived, but not necessarily the goal. These overlapping images provide an important message: Jesus is victorious over violence not because he rules with the sword, but because the sword does not rule him; he is victorious over it. Jesus finds a way of life rather than of death.[10]

This might seem an idealistic view in a world ravaged by violence, but plenty of real-life examples portray those who have sought solutions other than the use of force, including nonviolent resisters such as Gandhi and Martin Luther King Jr., but also the lesser known Desmond Doss. Doss, whose story is depicted in the biographical drama *Hacksaw Ridge*, refused to carry a weapon or kill enemy soldiers because of his Christian convictions, but nevertheless saved the lives of at least seventy-five of his comrades, repeatedly risking his own life and incurring injuries. Doss provides an example of how people in all areas of life, even the military, might act in ways that are nonviolent and simultaneously life-saving to others.

Resorting to violence represents a failure of the imagination, an attempt to relieve the pain of our wounds by creating more wounds that, in the end, only bring temporary relief. Dimitrios Pagourtzis, the alleged shooter at a high school in Santa Fe, Texas, killed ten people and wanted to kill himself. He was a lonely and awkward outsider who was embarrassed that one of his classmates had "rejected his advances."[11] Studies have shown that most school shootings are retributions for some kind of perceived injury caused by others: "A review of the targeted victims of the 48 shooters reveals a surprising pattern. School personnel (staff) and females were the most frequently targeted groups. In some cases, the perpetrators targeted specific individuals they knew, such as an ex-girlfriend. In other cases, females as a group were targeted. These results suggest that shooters were more enraged by teachers who failed them, administrators who disciplined them, and girls who rejected them than they were by peers who teased them."[12]

The perpetrators of these mass shootings seem to think that their problems could be solved by exacting revenge on those who have slighted them. But their violence only perpetuates pain for others and themselves; it cannot end pain.

At the time of this writing in 2018, since January 2009 there have been 288 school shootings in the United States, fifty-seven times the combined number of school shootings in all the other G7 countries (Canada, France, Germany, Italy, Japan, and the United Kingdom).[13] Violence has become the go-to solution in the United States for resolving problems, and firearms the instrument of choice. There is a deep disconnect between the ways our culture attempts to solve problems and our identity as a "Christian" nation. This is a narrative problem, one caused by cultural beliefs shaped by the myth of redemptive violence.

The story of Jesus' life in no way shows God seeking violence as the solution to difficulties, either social or cosmic. The image of the "violent God" that is apparently found in the Hebrew Scriptures must be moderated and reinterpreted by the life of Jesus. We must read accounts such as the Genesis flood and the oracles of the prophets in light of Jesus' embodiment of nonviolent resistance as revealed in the Gospels. Jesus is always reinterpreting his community's understanding of God. A violent and vindictive image of God only sows more violence into the soil of this land that was born of and is sustained by violence. Only the child, the Prince of Peace, can provide the shalom that we all seek.[14]

RESTORATIVE JUSTICE: RENEWAL FOR ALL CREATION

Some other societies have found solutions more effective than punitive justice:

> In the Babemba tribe of [southern] Africa, when a person acts irresponsibly or unjustly, he is placed in the center of the village, alone and unfettered. All work ceases, and every man, woman, and child in the village gathers in a large circle around the accused individual.
>
> Then each person in the tribe speaks to the accused, one at a time, each recalling the good things the person in the center of the circle has done in his lifetime. Every incident, every experience that can be recalled with any detail and accuracy, is recounted. All his positive attributes, good deeds, strengths, and kindnesses are recited carefully and at length. This tribal ceremony often lasts for several days. At the end, the tribal circle

is broken, a joyous celebration takes place, and the person is symbolically and literally welcomed back into the tribe.[15]

Restorative justice is the modus operandi sought by God throughout the Bible. God's restorative justice helps humanity and all of creation to become reconciled and whole, healed and united. Restorative justice confronts the violence and wrong actions of perpetrators, calling for repentance and action. The word *repentance*, so often associated with sorrow and contrition, means "a change of mind." Repentance might involve feelings of sorrow, but it also requires mental deconstruction that leads to transformative actions. In other words, it is not only being sorry, but changing behaviors so that one's life is also changed. It is to see all people as divine image bearers, and then living out this truth by treating all people as such. In reality, repentance is *good news* for perpetrators, because it provides the opportunity for them to exhibit "the mind of Christ" (1 Corinthians 2:16) rather than to operate from a kind of thinking that damages others and self. Within this new framework, oppressors can see others as made in the image of God and creation as an expression of God's love. They can see goodness and abundance in the universe, rather than scarcity. Repentance creates the possibility of embodied involvement, entering into community with others.

Restorative justice involves seeking ways in which perpetrators can be given opportunities to both understand the effects of their crimes and undergo restoration. "Sentencing circles" have been used in the prison systems in North America, especially in Canada, to reduce incarceration rates. Sometimes called peacemaking circles, these circles include an invitation to all parties involved to join a dialogue about what should be done in response to the harm done by an offender. The process of seeking restorative justice using a peacemaking circle involves: "(1) application by the offender to participate in the circle process; (2) a healing circle for the victim;

(3) a healing circle for the offender; (4) a sentencing circle to develop consensus on the elements of a sentencing plan; and (5) follow-up circles to monitor the progress of the offender."[16] In addition, these circles have been applied in schools in the United States to help young people deal with violations against others.[17]

As stated in chapter 5, the idea of punitive justice that we have in the United States is reaffirmed by punitive ways in which the Bible has been interpreted. However, this was not the way of the early church and the Eastern fathers who examined God's work in the world through the lens of restorative rather than punitive justice. Theologian Derek Flood, writing in response to those who interpret the early church's writing as affirming a penal substitutionary view of atonement, says that restorative justice

is restorative in the sense that salvation is focused on our healing and re-birth (restoring us), and restorative in that it seeks to overturn the system of death (restoring God's reign). This represents a paradigm of justice not based on a punitive model, but one focused on setting us right by transforming us, and setting the world right by overthrowing "the law of sin and death" (Ro 8:2). In this later sense it reflects a model of justice that is in fact the *opposite* of retributive justice, because it seeks ultimately to abolish retribution, not to appease it.[18]

If Christians continue to espouse, support, and disseminate the idea of God's punitive actions, then we can expect a continued cycle of hurt rather than healing. Doing so continues to appease the god of wrath while overlooking the ones who most seem to need to act out of vengeance—humans. Often, those who want God to be punitive are seeking permission to pursue their own desires to be punitive.

Restorative justice is directed toward the *han*-ridden and tends the wounds of the oppressed by demonstrating that there is a way to address injustice other than a cycle of resentment, anger, and continued violence. Restorative justice seeks to offer a solution that advocates for the wounded and restores their dignity and wholeness. In this way, forgiveness can rightly be offered to the perpetrators.

During the sentencing of Dylann Roof for the shooting of nine people in Charleston, South Carolina, magistrate James B. Gosnell told the families of victims and the community of Charleston, "It's best to learn how to forgive." But this urging to forgive was out of place for those hurt by the shootings. (A few days after making this comment, Gosnell was replaced as chief magistrate.) Forgiveness was eventually given by many members of the Emanuel African Methodist Episcopal Church, but it was through *their own* process and in their own time. Roof seemed unaffected by the graciousness of the families of his victims. This forgiveness was not really for Roof; he did not care to receive it.[19] But forgiveness allowed the families to receive healing and wholeness. Roof was given the death penalty for committing federal hate crimes, the first death penalty ever imposed by the federal government for this kind of case. In refusing forgiveness, Roof's life ended in that courtroom, while the survivors needed to continue theirs.

DISTRIBUTIVE JUSTICE: CORRECTING THE SCALES

Distributive justice is the method by which justice takes place. Distributive justice seeks to identify inequities and make corrections. The birth of the church involves distributive justice, when church leaders sought to correct inequities in the distribution of bread among Hellenic Christian (Greek-speaking Jews) and Hebraic Christian (Aramaic-speaking Jews) widows (Acts 6). The disciples saw that because the Hellenist Jews were of the diaspora, those who returned from Greek-speaking regions, resources were not being shared equally with them. In response, they appointed

Greek-speaking, Jewish Christians to the role of deacons and gave them responsibility to make sure the widows of the Hellenists were not overlooked. The problem of scarcity is resolved within their community of faith through equal distribution.

Reflection on this story leads me to pose an important question: Does the church represent all those in the world equally, or does inequality take place because people are not equally represented?

Reparations are an aspect of distributive justice that seek to pay back what has been taken away. Starting on February 19, 1942, a few years after World War II began, the United States detained and seized the property of over one hundred thousand people of Japanese ancestry living in the United Sates, many of whom were citizens. They were interned in concentration camps under the guise of national security. The same situation occurred in Canada, where twenty-two thousand Canadian citizens of Japanese descent were interned. In 1988 the Canadian government, under the leadership of prime minister Brian Mulroney, made a public apology and offered a package of financial redress to the families involved.

Also in 1988, U.S. president Ronald Reagan signed the Civil Liberties Act, sponsored by Congressman Norman Mineta, who was interned as a child at the Heart Mountain Relocation Center in Wyoming, and Senator Alan K. Simpson. The bill provided reparations of $20,000 for each surviving detainee, totaling $1.2 billion.

In 1942, Fred Korematsu, a Japanese American man living in San Leandro, California, refused to be forcibly relocated and was arrested for doing so. He fought his conviction all the way to the Supreme Court. But in 1944, the Supreme Court, in *Korematsu v. United States*, ruled that Korematsu was in violation of the law and that the United States acted lawfully in attempting to intern him and all other Japanese Americans. Not until 2018 did the Supreme Court declare the 1944 decision to intern Japanese Americans to be "unlawful." In an opinion written by Chief Justice John Roberts, the court ruled, "The dissent's reference to *Korematsu*, however, affords this Court the opportunity to make express what is already obvious: *Korematsu* was gravely wrong the day it was decided, has been overruled in the court of history, and—to be clear—'has no place in law under the Constitution.'"[20]

This legal ruling was only offered *incidentally, obiter dictum,* when the Supreme Court compared *Korematsu v. United States* to *Trump v. Hawaii* as part of a ruling to uphold a travel ban issued by President Trump. History will judge if the latter case decision should also have been decided differently by the courts, and if there will be more dissenting opinions in the future.

Another aspect of distributive justice is the forgiveness of debts. The great economic disparity in the United States is coupled with the huge debts that burden the economically disadvantaged. Cash advance and payday lenders often prey on those who are already in debt and cannot pay off their loans. Studies show that these predatory lenders intentionally target renters earning less than $40,000 a year who do not have a four-year college degree, are separated or divorced, and are African American. The interest rates are astounding—from 400 percent APR to as much as 5,000 percent APR (including fees and other costs). Often the only qualification for these types of loans is a car title, or a similar proof of assets. If a loan recipient is unable to repay the loan with interest, the predatory lender may seize the loan recipient's automobile, creating difficulty with transportation to work, which contributes to an escalating cycle of debt.

The Jewish year of Jubilee provided opportunities for debt forgiveness, liberating those who had accumulated debt from financial burdens that could take a lifetime to repay. In our debt-rich U.S. economy, people not only need wage increases and employment opportunities to repay their debt burdens, but also need opportunities for educational debt and other types of loans to be paid off so

that they can contribute to society in other ways. Studies indicate
that people of color in this society have the greatest health issues,
and that these issues are related to financial stresses.[21] Relieving
these stresses would help the economy overall by eliminating many
expenses related to healthcare.

In the United States, terms like *welfare* are stigmatized and have
become associated with the myth that those who use them are "gam-
ing the system," taking advantage of and being a burden on the government. But government reporting shows that the same number
of Republican voters and Democratic voters use what are known as
"entitlement programs." These studies also reveal that the vast number of people who use these programs are white Americans, not mi-
norities.[22] The "welfare of the city" that Jeremiah (29:7) describes
is reflexive. When we invest in the good of the city, it returns good
to us. Jeremiah lived during a time when the siege of the Southern
Kingdom by the Babylonian Empire was upon him. He interpreted
these events as God's actions to undo the idolatry of God's people.
They had betrayed God, trusted in foreign powers and therefore
foreign gods, and used children as sacrifices (Jeremiah 7:30-34).
Even though it seemed that God was letting God's people suffer
under foreign rule, Jeremiah's message was that a new covenant, or
promise, was being created:

> The days are surely coming, says the LORD, when I will make a
> new covenant with the house of Israel and the house of Judah.
> It will not be like the covenant that I made with their ancestors
> when I took them by the hand to bring them out of the land of
> Egypt—a covenant that they broke, though I was their husband,
> says the LORD. But this is the covenant that I will make with the
> house of Israel after those days, says the LORD: I will put my law
> within them, and I will write it on their hearts; and I will be their
> God, and they shall be my people. No longer shall they teach
> one another, or say to each other, "Know the LORD," for they

shall all know me, from the least of them to the greatest, says the LORD; for I will forgive their iniquity, and remember their sin no more." (Jeremiah 31:31-34)[23]

Within this passage, forgiveness of sin and restoration are offered through a covenant that is "written on their hearts." This new covenant was realized in the life and ministry of Jesus. He embodies forgiveness and a new law that is inscribed in the hearts of God's people (Romans 2:15; Hebrews 10:16). Jesus' model prayer, the Lord's Prayer, reminds us of the practicality of understanding God's forgiveness of both the sins caused by others and the financial debt that others owe to us:

Luke 11:3-4	Matthew 6:11-12
Give us each day our daily bread.	Give us this day our daily bread.
And forgive us our sins,	And forgive us our debts,
for we ourselves forgive everyone indebted to us.[24]	as we also have forgiven our debtors.

In Jesus' world there was no difference between the spiritual and financial relationship of sin and debt. For him, the economy of the kingdom dealt with the well-being of all aspects of humanity, not only those that we would consider spiritual. Consequently, to take direction only from the spiritual and not from the economic aspects of the Gospels would mean reverting to the gnostic/Cartesian dualism that Christianity has fought so hard to expunge.

Justice means not only balancing the scales, but also correcting the scales that have been so imbalanced. We need to constantly ask questions about who makes the rules of the game, who makes the laws of this country. Societies have a limit to the amount of injustice they will tolerate before they resort to violent revolution against those who have held the power and privilege for too long.

The philosopher Karl Marx understood this well when he set out to describe his theory about class struggle. But we do not need to get to the point of economic meltdown to understand this, especially if we are to be a just and peaceful society. We need to see that when we attempt to correct the injustices for the few, we will bring justice for all.

JUSTICE AND THE HEALING OF *HAN*

Jesus of the East is the healer of *han* who heals the wounds of his people. In order to understand this aspect of Jesus, we must explore what healing might mean and must undo some misconceptions about how it takes place.

Christianity is caught within two extremes. At one end of the spectrum is the charismatic faith healing movement, a type of prosperity gospel. At the other end is a liberal Protestantism that spiritualizes healing and often rejects the notion of physical healing through divine intervention.

The more charismatic notion of healing can devolve into a type of magic act in which people come to God to be cured of ailments that are often not treatable by modern medicine. Charismatic faith healings ask believers to expect God to do the miraculous, often when they have no place to go for healing. These types of healings are especially common in economically disadvantaged communities where medical resources are lacking. Pentecostalism, one form of charismatic faith, has spread throughout South and Central America and Africa because its emphasis on physical healing seems to meet the felt needs of those populations.

One of the drawbacks of charismatic movements has to do with the expectations of the members and the rejection of other forms of medical treatments that might be of benefit. The idea that God will give people everything they want and will heal everyone on the basis of their faith fails for two reasons.

The first is that in the gospel stories, Jesus did not heal everyone who sought healing. In Mark 6, Jesus preached at the synagogue in his hometown and was rejected because he claimed that God's work of healing and liberation was also intended for people outside of Israel. The story ends by stating, "And he could do no deed of power there, except that he laid his hands on a few sick people and cured them" (Mark 6:5). This narrative implies a limit to what Jesus could do, or wanted to do, given his interaction with the people at Nazareth. Most gospel stories of healing portray differing approaches to healing people, such as the woman with an issue of blood (Matthew 9:20-22; Mark 5:25-34; Luke 8:43-48). This woman persisted in coming to Jesus and even dared to touch his garment amid a tightly packed crowd. Her tenacity and belief that an encounter with Jesus would bring healing helped to make this healing possible. Her actions reflect an intentional act to secure intentional healing, a blessing stolen. Another story of healing involves a paralyzed man who was brought to Jesus by fellow villagers so desperate to have the man healed that they dismantled the roof of the house where Jesus was staying in order to lower the man through it, allowing him to meet Jesus (Matthew 9:1-8; Mark 2:1-12; Luke 5:17-26). In this narrative, it appears to be not the man's faith but the faith of his community that healed him.

A second observation is that in the Gospels, healing appears to be based on more than one's absolute faith. One's belief that Jesus can heal is an important aspect of healing, but healing is not based solely on the faith of those seeking healing. In many New Testament stories, Jesus responds to the faith of others on behalf of the sick person, such as the Roman officer who asked that his servant be made well (Matthew 8:5-13; Luke 7:1-10). People who fail to receive healing should not conclude that their own lack of faith prevented it. Doing so reflects a one-sided understanding of healing that places blame and shame on those who are sick.

Lastly, any faith in healing by divine miracle should not replace medical remedies. If one needs medical care, then one should seek it. Traditional Western medicine and medical treatment are a gift from God for our benefit. Physicians who help us get well from illnesses heal by divine power, whether they realize this or not. A physician was once asked, "How do you heal people?" She replied, "I prescribe the medicine. I stitch up the wound. But I do not heal; God does." The Latin phrase *Natura sanat, medicus curats*, "The physician treats, but nature cures," conveys the same idea. Healing comes through a community of healing agents and not only through one pathway. We cannot abandon one form of treatment for another.

Western medicine is limited by the best science that we currently have. There are other forms of medicines and homeopathic cures not included within Western medicine. Eastern therapies that use acupuncture and herbs have been used for centuries and have helped many people. Medicine, in whatever form, and divine healing are not mutually exclusive. In contrast, much of Protestant liberalism rejects these forms of charismatic healing because of its intellectualist bias. Those who attend mainline Protestant churches tend to be wealthier, giving them access to traditional forms of healthcare. Their worship style is less emotive and emphasizes the teaching aspects of Jesus' ministry rather than the miraculous and therapeutic aspects. At the same time, these Protestant churches have been the pioneers of some of the greatest institutions of medicine we have today. The word *hospital* comes from the word *hospitality*, invoking welcome. Many hospitals have Christian origins and were birthed in church denominations. Unfortunately, many of these institutions that were formerly devoted to public health and charity have become privatized through corporate ownership and have often shunned the poor and needy.

Healing is a broad term that can encompass both bodily and emotional therapies. An acquaintance of mine who advocates for HIV treatment in the LGBTQ+ community was once invited by a friend to attend a healing service. This service was *not* the kind we expect from a showy televangelist, but simply a service in which people brought needs to the altar and received prayer from the community. My acquaintance was hesitant to go forward for prayer. "Don't you believe that God heals people?" his friend asked. "Not in that way," my acquaintance answered. Many people in liberal Protestant communities do not intellectually reject the idea of God healing people. Why could God not heal physical illnesses? Perhaps God could heal, but maybe not in the *way* that I would prefer to be healed. Within these types of communities, it is medical and therapeutic professionals who are most involved in the care of the body and mind, while priests or ministers are involved in healing the spiritual aspects of a person, with clear divisions between these disciplines.

Are we simply caught between these two divergent perspectives, or is there a third way? I believe that all healing is a miracle, whether it comes through a doctor, a faith healer, or a person's own individual prayers. Healing is miraculous in that it is an act of restoration of the cosmos, which does not come easily or without pain. Healing can occur through communities that intentionally provide opportunities for healing and health through preventative programs of diet and exercise, counseling programs, mentorships, food assistance, work training, and low-cost medical treatment. There are aspects of healing that can occur beyond physical healing, such as emotional, psychological, and behavioral healing. This kind of healing includes the restoration of relationships between oppressors and oppressed, healing for the victims of perpetrators, and healing that takes place with the land and resources.

In order to accomplish Jesus' vision of the kingdom, healing must be holistic and not only physical. Our goal should be the complete health of persons and communities. This kind of wholeness comes through the relationships that are formed when people engage in the kind of kinship described by Sara Miles in *Take This Bread*. Miles speaks of serving her community not only through food pantries and other enfleshed forms of ministry, but also through the liturgy of the St. Gregory of Nyssa Episcopal Church. There, the congregational worship mirrors the intermingling dance of the divine through the practice of dancing together in a line. Old and young, gay and straight, women and men, poor and rich, sinner and sin-ridden, all place a hand on each other's shoulder to dance around the church, a worship practice that is symbolic of the community's closely knit, interdependent, and not purely transactional relationships. Above the worshipers hang pictures of saints who are also intertwined in their own dance of worship. The kingdom exists in these relationships, and health, healing, and well-being emerge from this kind of community, which mirrors the community of God.

The Eastern fathers passed down an image of God that is termed *perichoretic*. Put simply, it is an image of an intermingling dance.[25] A perichoretic image of God envisions an intimate relationship of oneness expressed in Jesus' prayer of unity: "That they may all be one. As you, Father, are in me and I am in you, may they also be one in us, so that the cosmos may trust that you have sent me" (John 17:21, translation mine). Because God contains diversity within God's very self, this understanding of God reflects a community with God characterized by unity of differences and unity *in* differences. It is in this kind of community that healing can occur.

In my own life and communities, I have struggled with the healthcare system, sometimes because I did not have health insurance, especially when I was a student or working part-time as a college professor. At other times my family has benefited from government-subsidized healthcare, but more often than not, my wife and I have had to pay out of pocket because we lacked health insurance as a result of being underemployed, full-time students, or self-employed. Once we were both very ill, to the point that my wife (my fiancée at the time) had pneumonia. A physician friend came to our aid, providing medical care for my wife and averting a trip to the emergency department. I wonder how many families do not have friends or family who can help in this way. It is ironic that this nation of prosperity, a nation that can put a person on the moon and split the atom to create energy, cannot provide universal healthcare for its own people, and especially those who helped build it.

CREATING COMMUNITIES OF HEALING

Augustine expresses the Trinity in relationship between the lover, beloved, and love:[26]

Figure 2. The relationship of love

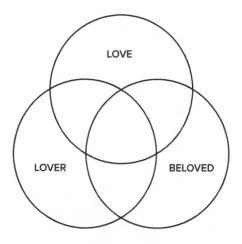

For Augustine, God is found in this analogy of love's entanglement. German theologian Jürgen Moltmann expands the idea, using the language of "forsakenness":

Figure 3. The relationship of forsakenness

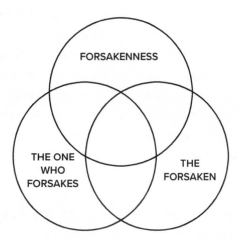

Han can be added to these depictions of the triune nature of God:

Figure 4. The relationship of han

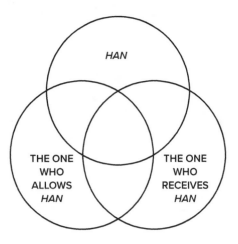

If we visualize God as this intermingling dance of love, abandonment, and woundedness, we can understand the ways in which communities can find healing through the intersection of each other's wounds with the strength of the Spirit of God, who heals those wounds.

The Father/Mother/Parent God is the one who allows *han*, not because this person of God inflicts *han* on others, but because they are open to receiving and transforming the *han* of the world. The divine Parent gives their Son to the world and is open to letting this Son suffer woundedness, just as the divine Parent is open to the Son experiencing forsakenness. Radical love requires allowing the ones you love to experience hurt instead of trying to protect them from all hurt. In an age of helicopter parenting, we know that those who seek to overprotect and smother their children rob them of precious life experiences. Within reason, children need to experience hurt and to learn how to appropriately seek attention for their own wounds and the wounds of others. They need to know that their parents will be there for them, but do not need the constant protection from all possible sources of woundedness.

The Son/Daughter/Child of God is characterized by *han* because this person of the Godhead is not only open to being hurt but also has taken on hurt. This woundedness of God invites us to confront the ways in which we have wounded God and all that is good and beautiful in the world. God's woundedness shows how we have wounded others through our own personal acts and by participating in acts of systemic oppression toward others. The Spirit becomes the wound itself, the connection between the Parent and Child. The Spirit is the open sore of all the pain in the world. The Spirit is the hurt that the Father experiences in the loss of the Son, and the Spirit is the pain that the Son suffers in being given to this world. In being the nexus of suffering, the Spirit becomes the wounded healer, able to restore and bring unity to the community of hurt.

Protest movements such as Me Too and Black Lives Matter bring to the forefront hurt that others have inflicted. Black Lives Matter highlights the disproportional police shootings directed at African Americans and other people of color. A recent report shows that people of color represent 38.5 percent of the population, but 51.5 percent of all "years of life lost" in 2015 and 2016. However, in 2018, fatal police shootings in general declined, falling below 1,000 deaths.[27] This was down from 1,146 police killings in 2015 and 1,092 in 2016. Whether movements such as Black Lives Matter have contributed to this decline remains to be seen. Organizations like these have pressed for cultural awareness training for police officers and the mandatory use of police body cameras in some districts, but some police departments still have not had training in solutions other than those involving violent force.

Although these movements confront problems that cause harm, they fail to address the need to provide healing for victims. This healing may come in the form of support and education from communities. In the South, church buildings were often constructed on the sites of "hush arbors." These were meeting places where enslaved people would secretly congregate to worship and find peace. The only legal and allowable form of religion for them was the one of their captors. However, these enslaved people identified with the narrative of Jesus' suffering and his liberative ministry, providing hope and solace in harsh conditions. Safe places like these hush arbors need to be created for victims who suffer from *han*. Those who have suffered harm need places to talk to others and receive treatment for their injuries so that their wounds do not fester and cause harm to others. In the end, people are never just victims *or* just perpetrators. Some perpetrators are themselves victims who need healing. At the very least, those who commit crimes against others need viable strategies for reformation. Accountability and rehabilitation go hand in hand, otherwise the cycle of *han* will continue. Healing requires access both to places of safety and to places of resistance. Moving in and out of these places is the difficult and rewarding work of true community.

We also need to encourage and nurture what Christian environmental activist Larry Rasmussen terms "anticipatory communities,"[28] places in which people live out a vision of how the world *should be* instead of only talking about what they want it to become. Too often, seminarians are taught the already/not yet dialectic of the kingdom of God as a way of making peace with the fact that the kingdom has yet to arrive. The implication is that we should wait passively for its arrival. But why wait? Many people who suffer injustice cannot wait until some future relief comes. Others who have benefited from the status quo need to be alerted to the reality that this fragile system, which depends on being continually fed at the expense of those who are harmed, will soon topple. If those who benefit from the current system do not work toward redemptive, restorative justice, the benefits will no longer flow their way. However, when all work toward the goals of restoration, all will benefit.

One story of a perpetrator who changed his mind and life is the story of Ken Parker, who attended the Unite the Right rally in Charlottesville, Virginia, in August 2017, where thirty-two-year-old Heather Heyer was run down by a driver who was part of the neo-Nazi movement.[29] At the rally, Parker became weary from heat exhaustion. He was wearing a dark-colored white nationalist uniform and was dehydrated. Deeyah Khan, a Muslim woman from Norway who was also a documentary filmmaker, saw Parker's distress, had compassion on him, and approached Parker to ensure that he was cared for. Because of that experience, Parker was transformed from a man who spewed hatred for Black, gay, and Jewish people. He began to question his beliefs about race. "That kind of got me thinking," Parker said. "She's a really nice lady. Just because she's got darker skin and believes in a different god than the god I believe in, why am I hating these people?"[30]

A few months later, Parker saw a group of African Americans at a barbecue near his apartment. He met the organizer of the event and struck up a conversation. Parker did not know it at the time, but the man he was speaking with was also a pastor at a predominantly African American church. Parker was invited to the church. When he visited, to his surprise, Parker was asked to come up front to give a testimony. When he told the audience that he was a former Klansman and neo-Nazi, "jaws dropped," but after his testimony, everyone came up to thank and hug him. Parker was later baptized by this congregation and now helps those who are seeking ways out of hate groups.

Parker, like others who have made this move, crossed a line that divided people between the oppressed and the oppressor. Khan, in her act of compassion and empathy, reached out to an enemy to care for his needs, even though she had every right to refuse to do so. Because of this act of creative healing, Parker and others have sought to repent of their ways of thinking and acting and are now helping others to do the same. Reconciliation came about when they sought unity with others, which also brought about reconciliation with themselves, God, and the world. This work could not happen without the context of a community. This kind of healing is much more than the work of one church or one denomination—it is the work of the kingdom.

Both Deeyah Khan and Parker's church community demonstrated a response to *han* that is reflected in the Korean term *dan*. *Dan*, meaning "to cut off," draws its imagery from Korean poet of protest Chi-Ha Kim, and consists of personal and social dimensions.[31] On a personal level, *dan* involves self-denial; it is the resistance to revenge and violence against the oppressors. On the social level, *dan* involves the act of cutting off the cycle of violence, without which *han* would continue, and which prevents the oppressed from lashing out. Practicing *dan* does not mean that the oppressed do not have strategies for change. By responding with *dan*, the wounded can position themselves in ways that are transformative to others, and which also promote healing for themselves. This is the value of life together. People help each other actualize *dan* in order to promote social change. The ripples of healing and reconciliation move outward to counter the tide of wounding and woundedness in the world.

German theologian Dietrich Bonhoeffer saw the kingdom as calling us to reach out into the world and to not remain within the insulated confines of church. Before he was executed in a Nazi concentration camp, Bonhoeffer hoped to write a book about "Christianity without religion." In a time when the value of words was being diminished and people no longer believed in the arguments of religious and political leaders, Bonhoeffer saw that Christ could no longer be contained within an institution. Bonhoeffer alluded to this idea in *Letters and Papers from Prison*: "[God] must be recognized at the centre of life, not when we are at the end of our resources; it is [God's] will to be recognized in life, and not only when death comes; in health and vigor, and not only in suffering; in our activities, and not only in sin. The ground for this lies in the revelation of God in Jesus Christ."[32]

If God is to be meaningful, it cannot be as only the "God of the gaps" who offers an explanation for the problems that science cannot explain. For Bonhoeffer, God must be more than that—otherwise, when science provides answers for our questions, God ceases to be relevant. In addition, Bonhoeffer believed that Christianity cannot simply be a source for solutions to spiritual questions about postmortem existence and guilt. Instead, the God of Christianity can be revealed in all aspects of life

The kingdom is not about privatized religion. Rather, the kinship of God is spreading throughout the world through extraordinary people who attempt to do courageous things at the risk of their own personal welfare, as well as through very ordinary people seeking, in their everyday circumstances, to be faithful to the vision that Jesus taught and lived. Those who are citizens of this kingdom seek to create spaces where the *han*-ridden can find both healing for their wounds and comfort in one another. They seek to help people engage in acts of forgiveness and find solutions that restore others to be the persons they were created to be, in the image of God. The territory of the kingdom appears in places that might not even seem religious in nature, but that reveal God's intent for the world, spaces where sinners and the sinned-against meet. These are the places that Christ inhabits, the places of *han*.

BETWEEN FORGETTING AND REMEMBERING

As the plane took off from Saigon (Hồ Chí Minh City), the former capital of South Vietnam, I found myself dwelling on my memories of a land that had attempted to heal through forgetfulness and time. Other than our tour of the Củ Chi tunnels, where Viet Cong soldiers had dug hundreds of miles of tunnels in which to live and fight, and various war monuments where we had gone sightseeing, we had seen few signs of a civil war. The war seemed to be only an imagining. As the older generation passes, there will soon be no trace. Just as only a handful can read the ancient Vietnamese writings of Chữ Nôm, so only a few remaining survivors will continue to retell the stories, and Vietnam will continue to build on top of the destruction and desolation. But the existence of the war and its memories are as entangled as the lines of electrical and telephone wire in Hà Nội, a snarled web of old and new. The struggle we face now is between memory and forgetfulness, and we cannot know who we are if we forget. Writer Viet Thanh Nguyen reflects: "Our ambivalence about war's identity simply expresses ambivalence about our own identities, which are collectively inseparable from the wars our nations have fought. These are the wars for which we have paid, from which we have benefitted, by which we are traumatized. Whatever may be noble and heroic in war is found in us, and whatever is evil and horrific in war is also found in us."[33]

In many ways, all those who read this book are the product of conflict—none of us are born from a void; rather, we emerge from the mire of history and its battles. The history of the United States is a story about birth through war and about the wars we continue to fight, whether on foreign soil or on our own. This story of ongoing conflict seems inescapable. Our failure to remember and come to grips with this history is also our failure to know who we are as people.

There is also a war at the forefront of Christian faith. This war is fought for the identity of Jesus. Much about Jesus has been lost over two millennia. This struggle might not be relevant if Christianity had simply come and gone, dying off like an ancient myth. But retellings of the Jesus story in the lives of people who have encountered this Jesus persist. These stories tenaciously continue because people are still befriending this Jesus. Some retellings are gentle, tender, transformative, and worthy of the Nazarene rabbi, but others repeat the story of conquest and empire, of a Christianity that colonized and continues to colonize. Those stories are stories of "Jesus" in name only because they are incompatible with the story that was handed down to us by the first Christians. In many ways, those stories are not a remembering of Jesus, but rather require the active forgetting of Jesus.

Somewhere on Marble Mountain in Đà Nẵng, Vietnam, my ancestors are buried. My cousin tells stories of soldiers who, after fighting wars, returned to civilian life to live out the rest of their years as Buddhist monks, even though they could have married and had children. This is the story of my ancestors. Perhaps the only way they could purge the trauma of war that raged within them was through a life of solitude and detachment. In the misty fog of the mountains, they found their rest.

But their struggles continue in my own life. A war still stirs in my heart, a war made up of many memories, many stories, and not enough words. Often, I hesitate to tell the story that I should tell. At times, the pressure of my own life, my own struggle to survive and provide for my family, keeps me from narrating the story of a Jesus who was also conflicted by his past and identity, by trauma and the self. I have no fantastic tales of miracles, no exciting testimonies of radical transformation, only encounters with my own recollections that seep into my present, understandings of who I am in light of what has happened. My identity is entrenched in a war that began before my birth, a war that has brought me here to these United States. My identity is also shaped by the culture that presently exists in the West, a culture that is formed by its religious and political past. If I pull all these threads apart, I will also pull myself apart. I cannot escape these memories. So I come back to the same places again and again, returning to the washing of wounds in the waters—not the waters of Dante's Lethe, so as to forget, but to remember.

Memories, even good memories, often hurt. But they can reveal that not everything is lost to us. They may open us up to joy. They can help us learn from our past and shape our futures. The exceedingly good news of the Jesus of the East is that he does not simply live in the archival memories of an ancient tradition, in painted icons or ancient texts, but dwells in the lives of those who are living today. Encountering Jesus brings us freedom by connecting us to what matters most, the love that exists between all of us, the love without which we would not have this universe of people and places, of creation and being.

TIMELINE OF NOTED EVENTS

c. 30 CE ○ **Apostolic church**

c. 100 with earlier origins ○ **Gnosticism**

64–68 ○ **Persecution of Christians under Emperor Nero**

c. 100–700 ○ **The early Eastern fathers**
Ransom and recapitulation views of atonement

272–337 ○ **Constantine I**
Christianity becomes the state religion

354–430 ○ **Augustine of Hippo**
Original sin

1033/34–1109 ○ **Anselm of Canterbury**
Satisfaction view of atonement

1509–1564 ○ **John Calvin**
Penal substitutionary view of atonement

1596–1650 ○ **René Descartes**
Meditations on First Philosophy

c. 1600–1800 ○ **Western slave trade**

1861–1865 ○ **American Civil War**

1870s–1960s ○ **Jim Crow laws**

1950–1953 ○ **Korean War**

1955–1975 ○ **American (Vietnam) War**

1970s ○ **Emergence of Minjung theology**

1923–2015 ○ **René Girard**
Scapegoat mechanism

2013 ○ **Black Lives Matter movement**

2017 ○ **Me Too movement (with earlier origins)**

ACKNOWLEDGMENTS

I am indebted to those who first helped me formulate my thoughts around these ideas and also helped me live them out: Dr. Andrew Sung Park and Dr. Brad Jersak; also, Dr. Bob Eckblad, whose work with those at the margins I find myself constantly admiring and who connected me to Brad Jersak. To the first community where I presented these ideas, with gratitude for their invaluable feedback: Kelley Burd-Huss, McKenzie Watson, Rev. Greg Taylor, Rev. Tommie and Shorna Anderson. Thank you, Rev. Tommy Williams, for providing space and a listening ear to help me do this work.

My first readers endured revision after revision and constant questioning about how to make this work better: Rev. Julius Wardley, Rev. John Norwood, and Rozella Haydée White. Rev. Marty Troyer directed me to Herald Press. A special shout-out goes to Nate Dickerson, who engaged the text like it was his own life's work. Cheers.

All those who support me in the literary community in Houston: Mark Dostert, Daniel Peña, D. F. Brown, Chris Cander, Cameron

Dezen Hammon, and the students of the University of Houston and Rice University. The Between the Bayous Book Club: Lisa, Pam, Rob, Frank, and John Hayes. Words matter.

To Brazos Bookstore and the family there: Mark, Ülrika, Traci, Keaton, and all the friendly and helpful staff. Buy indie.

My crew, who embody the love of Jesus in ways enumerable and immeasurable: Sarah, Sanjiv, Juliet, Ray, Georgeann, Jesse, and Todd. Family.

The good people at Herald Press: Amy Gingerich, who first contacted me about the project and quickly became excited about the prospect of collaborating on a work that would last beyond a one-year book cycle. Dayna Olson-Getty, for the editorial work and insights. I could not have chosen a better editor, one who added tremendously to the work. And all the people from marketing to sales, from graphic design to line edits, it's *our* work. Peace.

Episcopal High School, Houston, gave me the opportunity to return to education after a long sabbatical for writing. There, I felt like a distinguished professor who was given time to both teach and write. And where religion and English live together, literally. Special thanks to Bishop Andrew Doyle for his help to get me there. Knights.

Dr. Jessica Cole helped me with the all-important query letter and initial edit of the synopsis, without which this project would have fallen flat. Shalom.

My writing partner, Kate Martin Williams, sat by me as I wrote this work, giving me feedback, asking tough questions, presenting helpful perspectives, and laughing at my lame jokes. Moving from theology to literature would not be possible without her. Together.

Last, but most importantly, without the support of Paula Nguyen Luu, my wife, I could not have produced this work. Her sacrifices carry this book. Love.

NOTES

INTRODUCTION

1. The history of the Eastern Orthodox Church is also one of political appropriation by Emperor Constantine I, who set up Byzantium, or Constantinople, in the East as the center of Roman power in 330 CE. This led to the Great Schism of 1054, which created the East/West divisions in the church. The eventual collapse of Constantinople in the Ottoman Empire testifies to the fragility of relationship between political power and the church.
2. "The Holy Eucharist: Rite 2," in the Book of Common Prayer, 360. To the credit of the Episcopal Church, at least some of the psalms, if not the theology, in the back of the Book of Common Prayer lend themselves to the prayers of the sinned-against.
3. Lonergan, *Papers 1958–1964*, 3–14.

CHAPTER 1

1. Nguyen, *Nothing Ever Dies*, 17.
2. Although I am not a sports fan, the Houston Astros' winning of the World Series in 2017 was a momentous time for Houston after the catastrophic events of Hurricane Harvey just months before. Sadly, in 2019, the team was found to have engaged in "sign stealing," violating baseball rules and calling their 2017 victory into question.
3. Origen, *Contra Celsum*.
4. This is a riff on the title of Alasdair MacIntyre's book *Whose Justice? Which Rationality?*, which discusses ethics.
5. There are many articles about "nones": those without religious affiliations, but who do not see themselves as atheists. See, for example, Shermer, "Americans without Religious Affiliation."

6. Ironically, Paul was never a disciple of Jesus in the flesh. He only had a vision of the resurrected Christ. Paul was also a Pharisee, a legal expert, who read the Scriptures through the eyes of the Jewish law. However, to Paul's credit, his mission was to convert not his own people, who largely rejected his message, but the Greeks, those the Jews considered the "uncircumcised" and "sinners." He grew beyond his own culture to embrace something that was not his own, even under the threat of persecution and death.

7. "Si comprehendis non est Deus," translation mine. Augustine, Sermon 117. For the English, see *Sermon on the Mount; Harmony of the Gospels; Homilies on the Gospels*, trans. R. G. MacMullen, vol. 6 of *Nicene and Post-Nicene Fathers*, Series 1, ed. Philip Schaff (Grand Rapids, MI: Eerdmans), 963.

8. Dick, *Man in the High Castle*.

9. Michel Martin, "Slave Bible from 1800s."

CHAPTER 2

1. Emerson and Smith, *Divided by Faith*.

2. U.S. Census Bureau, "About Race."

3. Somashekhar, "Undertreated for Pain."

4. Wallis, *America's Original Sin*.

5. Anselm, *Why God Became Man* 1.25.

6. Athanasius, *De Incarnatione* 54.10, translation mine. Cf. Irenaeus, "Word of God, our Lord Jesus Christ, who did, through His transcendent love, become what we are, that He might bring us to be even what He is Himself" (*Against Heresies* 5.preface).

7. This is evident in many works of Plato, but *The Republic* especially demonstrates this in the sections on education in book 7.

8. In recent years there has been a resurgence of interest in Gnosticism and alternative versions of the Gospels (see the work of Elaine Pagels). I do not deny the value of this literature and would encourage anyone to read and study it, but I am attempting here to outline a history of how the enfleshment of Jesus has ceased to be.

9. *Meditations on First Philosophy* was published in the Latin as *Meditationes de prima philosophia, in qua Dei existentia et animæ immortalitas demonstratur* and in the translated French as *Méditations métaphysiques*. "First philosophy" is an adage used by philosophers to denote what is studied primarily in philosophy, i.e., being. This was also called metaphysics. Descartes sought to start his first philosophy with the demonstrations for the existence of God and the immortality of the soul. However, these "demonstrations" sought independence from any type of bodily existence deductions from nature.

10. In Latin, "Cogito, ergo sum." In the original version of *Meditations*, the (translated) phrase is "I think, therefore I exist."

11. National Center for Chronic Disease Prevention and Health Promotion (US) Office on Smoking and Health, *Health Consequences of Smoking*.

12. See Hannam, *Genesis of Science*.

13. Lee and Park, "15 Black Lives Ended."

14. See Viet Thanh Nguyen's project *An Other War Memorial*, http://anotherwarmemorial.com, in which he and his students question why certain national memo-

rials honor U.S. soldiers who participated in the wars, but not others who died. The total body count of Vietnamese people, both combatants and civilians, have been projected to be closer to 3.8 million, making it 20 percent of the population of Vietnam at that time. However, records are difficult to come by because of inaccurate and incomplete reporting during the war.

15. Ignatius, *To the Smyrnaeans* 2.

16. Ross, *The Grief of God*, 6.

17. Williams, *Bonhoeffer's Black Jesus*, 3.

18. Irenaeus, *Against Heresies*, 2.22.4. It is a curiosity to note that Irenaeus includes old age because he believes that, based on the account of John the evangelist, Jesus was crucified at the age of fifty. Steenberg, *Of God and Man*, 44n67.

19. Gregory of Nazianzus, "Ep. 101 (To Cledonius)."

20. "Face to face" can be also translated "lip to lip" (Hebrew *pel el pel*), which points not only to the intimacy between God and Moses, but also to the bodily relationship that they shared. Men in the Near and Middle East would not be averse to kissing each other on the lips when greeting. In the West, especially the United States, these expressions of bodily contact between men are often questioned.

21. This idea of a "migratory God" is based on Fr. Daniel G. Groody's work on the theology of migration.

CHAPTER 3

1. The name Pharisee comes from the Hebrew and then Greek word that means "separatist."

2. Park, *Triune Atonement*, 44–45.

3. "Praise be God he has not created me a gentile; praise be God that he has not created me a woman; praise be God that he has not created me an ignorant man" (Tosefta Berakhot 7.8).

4. Augustine and his contemporaries believed (incorrectly) that biological inheritance came exclusively through fathers, while mothers provided only the fertile environment of the womb (seen as analogous to a fertile field) in which the father's seed would grow.

5. Augustine admits to his difficulty with reading the Greek language in his *Confessions*: "Why then did I hate Greek which has similar songs to sing? Homer was skilled at weaving such stories, and with sheer delight mixed vanity. Yet to me as a boy he was repellent. I can well believe that Greek boys feel the same about Virgil when they are forced to learn him in the way that I learnt Homer. The difficulty lies there: the difficulty of learning a foreign language at all. It sprinkles gall, as it were, over all the charm of the stories the Greeks tell. I did not know any of the words, and violent pressure on me to learn them was imposed by means of fearful and cruel punishments." Augustine, *Confessions* 14.2.

6. Madoff, "Statement to the Court." Madoff's other son later died of mantle cell lymphoma at the age of forty-eight.

7. Pelagius, *To Demetrias* 16.2.

8. In a court of law, a crime is evaluated in terms of the act, the intention (motive), and the circumstance. All these aspects contribute to an assessment of how much culpability or free will is involved in the crime. The U.S. criminal justice system is based on these standards of free will, and it is quite amazing that certain sections of

Christian religion and certain sections of other religions deny these elements alto-gether.

9. "Synod against the Heresy of Pelagius and Celestius," in Percival, ed., *Seven Ecumenical Councils*, 496. Regarding original sin and the baptism of infants, this synod was ratified by the seven ecumenical councils (Latin Canon 108; Greek Canon 112). However, even to this day, the Eastern Orthodox Church rejects the doctrine of original sin and instead promotes the doctrine of "ancestral sin," which places the guilt of Adam and Eve on the first couple and not all of humanity. What is passed on is instead the consequence for the sin, which is death, and the shame that comes from it.

10. It is ironic that the words *heresy* and *heretic* come from Latin and Greek words that mean "to choose" and "choice," respectively. In other words, one is a heretic when there are choices to be made and sides to join. However, Augustine's contention with Pelagius is that human choice is corrupted in the first place without God's grace. But this leaves us asking, What real choice is there to make?

11. The Lutheran priest Gustaf Aulén popularized this theory in his book *Christus Victor*, first published in English in 1931.

12. Other versions of this theory emerged over time, including a riff on this theory by the Mennonite theologian J. Denny Weaver in the twenty-first century. See Weaver, *Nonviolent Atonement*, regarding what he calls "narrative Christus Victor."

13. "For our struggle is not against enemies of blood and flesh, but against the rulers, against the authorities, against the cosmic powers of this present darkness, against the spiritual forces of evil in the heavenly places" (Ephesians 6:12).

14. Based on Robert Alter's translation in *Genesis*, 5.

15. The phrases *besalmenu* (in our image) and *kidmutenu* (according to our likeness) could be a product of Hebrew parallelism in poetry, but the Eastern fathers, who were more versed in Greek and Latin, understood these meanings differently.

16. See Park, *Triune Atonement*; and Park, "The Bible and *Han*." Also, for a Catholic perspective, see Considine, *Salvation for the Sinned-Against*.

17. Paul sought to write a systematic theology of sin as much as the sum of my social media posts constitute a dissertation on any one topic. This was not to say that Paul did not have anything important to say, but it is doubtful he believed that his letters would live to the twenty-first century and be analyzed, interpreted, debated, and translated by scholars.

18. Anselm, *Why God Became Man* 1.11.

19. Calvin, *Institutes of Christian Religion* 2.1.8.

20. The name Adam is derived from the Hebrew word *adama*, meaning "earth."

21. Few theologians outside of Minjung theology, such as Kevin Considine in the Catholic tradition, have become aware of this problem. See Considine, *Salvation for the Sinned-Against*.

22. The United States was tangled in conflict with Korea long before the Korean War. A U.S. expedition to Korea in 1871 resulted in the Battle of Ganghwa.

23. Other scholars, such as Andrew Sung Park, have also made this connection. See Park, *Racial Conflict and Healing*, 11.

24. Park, "The Bible and *Han*," 48.

25. "Read Obama's Full Speech from the University of Illinois," NBC Chicago, September 8, 2018, https://www.nbcchicago.com/blogs/ward-room/obama-university-of-illinois-full-speech-492719531.html.

26. Federal Bureau of Investigations, "2017 Hate Crime Statistics."

27. I use the term Judeo-Christian loosely, because many of the founding fathers of this country were not Christians in the traditional sense, but deists who believed in a non-involved, watchmaker-type god.

28. See the work of Michael Emerson in *Market Cities, People Cities: The Shape of Our Urban Future*.

29. The word that I translate as "rethink" comes from the Greek word *metanoia*, meaning to change one's heart or mind. The word *repent* has the loaded connotation of turning from sin, which might be the case if sin is described as I have described it in this book, rather than as some sort of violation of moral code. Some scholars have chosen to translate this term "conversion" and "conversion of mind" seems an appropriate alternative translation.

30. Davis, "Midland Voices: Graveyard in the Clouds."

CHAPTER 4

1. I.e., the feeding of the five thousand (Matthew 14:13-21; Mark 6:31-44; Luke 9:12-17; John 6:1-14) and the feeding of the four thousand (Matthew 15:32-39; Mark 8:1-9).

2. Thomas, *Summa theologiae* 1.104.1.ad 4. It is indeed interesting to note that even though everyone from Augustine up to Aquinas spoke of *creatio continua* (continued creative acts), John Calvin removes this from his theology and only speaks of the first act of creation in terms of *creatio ex nihilo* (creation out of nothing).

3. Park, "Minjung Theology," 2.

4. This is a common theme in the work of Walter Brueggemann, but a helpful article is Brueggemann, "Liturgy of Abundance."

5. The name *manna* comes from the Hebrew word *manhu*, meaning "what is it?"

6. Bass, "Table of Gifts."

7. The Last Supper event is depicted in all four Gospels and points to how this ritual was enacted and remembered by the early church.

8. I would direct readers to Michelle Alexander's excellent work, *The New Jim Crow: Mass Incarceration in an Age of Colorblindness*, which talks about these issues in depth.

9. Wallis, *America's Original Sin*.

10. The terms *racist* and *white supremacist* should not be taken as slurs, but descriptors. They describe not who people are, but their actions and attitudes. People who seek to change these attitudes and behaviors then become less racist toward others. Ibram Kendi writes that a word like *racist* "is descriptive, and the only way to undo racism is to consistently identify and describe it—and then dismantle it. The attempt to turn this usefully descriptive term into an almost unusable slur is, of course, designed to do the opposite: to freeze us into inaction." Kendi, *How to Be an Antiracist*, 9.

11. Jones, "Allegories on Race and Racism."

12. There are two distinct creation stories in Genesis, the first in 1:1–2:4a and the second in 2:4b-3. If one reads these sections separately, then one can see the differ-

ences in the order of creation and the uses of the name of God (YHWH or LORD). These two stories show the distinct voices of these writers and what they sought to convey about creation.

13. MacIntyre, *Dependent Rational Animals*.

14. Rape, Abuse, and Incest National Network, "Campus Sexual Violence: Statistics."

15. Reports of marijuana use among college males, Ross and DeJong, "Drug Use and Abuse."

16. A former Baylor University fraternity president, Jacob Walter Anderson, was indicted on four counts of sexual assault of a nineteen-year-old female student but received no prison time thanks to a plea deal with the McLennan County district attorney.

17. Kendi, "Frat and a Gang?"

18. This is not to say that fraternities are inherently good or bad, but to shed light on the lack of policing of fraternities in contrast to the policing of African American and Latinx communities. Of course, there are also African American fraternities, especially at historically Black colleges and universities, or HBCUs.

19. Clement of Alexandria, *The Stromata* 2.7.

20. Irenaeus, *Against Heresies*, 4.41.2.

21. Ibid., 4.37.2.

22. Middleton, *Liberating Image*, 297.

23. Harper, *Very Good Gospel*, 31.

24. Ekblad, *Bible with the Damned*, 179–96.

25. Hardin, "Christianity Is Changing." Also, Hardin and others talk much about non-violent redemption in Jersak and Hardin, eds., *Stricken by God?*

26. For an overview of atonement models, see Park, *Triune Atonement*; and Jersak, *A More Christlike God*. Beilby and Eddy, eds., *Nature of Atonement*, provide perspectives to the various sides of the debate. This is just to name a few. Of late, droves of books have been written on the topic, but I note again that all views, including my own, are metaphors and images that have been made into theories and doctrines. To be overly dogmatic would do an injustice to the imagery they are seeking to convey.

CHAPTER 5

1. Piper, "Is God Less Glorious?" If by "glorious" Piper means "able to be worshiped" (which I think he does in his quoting of Job), then I would answer yes, because then what would be the difference between God and a violent lunatic? According to Piper, nothing, I suppose.

2. The Anthony Graves Foundation. Graves's story can be found in Graves, *Infinite Hope*.

3. Gorringe, *God's Just Vengeance*.

4. For various views of atonement theories, see Tidball, Hilborn, and Thacker, eds., *Atonement Debate*; and, as noted earlier, Beilby and Eddy, eds., *Nature of Atonement*. However, for a helpful view forward in the debate, see Jersak, *A More Christlike God*.

5. Thomas, *Summa theologiae* 3.Q.46.A1–2. Here Thomas defines "necessity" in two ways to clarify what is meant by these terms.

6. Girard, *The Scapegoat*; Williams, *Bible, Violence, and the Sacred*.

7. Wink, *Powers That Be*.

8. Irenaeus, *Against Heresies* 5.21.1.

9. Ekblad, *Bible with the Damned*.

10. Le Guin, "Ones Who Walk Away."

11. According to a financial report by Gohringer, "Cost of the Crisis." However, the eventual cost might be closer to $20 trillion.

12. I will not explore each point of Ekblad's thesis, but the reader is encouraged to read the very convincing argument that he has outlined in "God Is Not to Blame," in Jersak and Hardin, eds., *Stricken by God?*, 180–204.

13. Calarco, "Suffering Servant of Isaiah 53."

14. Ibid.

15. Ekblad, "God Is Not to Blame," 196.

16. Augustine, *De Trinitate* 9.1.1.

17. Thomas, *Summa theologiae*, 3.Q46.A5, co.; 3.Q50.A2.ad.1.

18. Moltmann, *Crucified God*, 229–30.

19. Or as I like to call it, "The story of the father, the older son, and the younger son," but this will never receive any airtime. For a wonderful reflection on all three characters, see Nouwen, *Return of the Prodigal*.

20. See Richards and O'Brien's *Misreading Scripture with Western Eyes*, which illustrates a fascinating point as to how readers, depending on their cultural backgrounds, remember or do not remember the account of the famine in this story.

21. In previous stories, Jesus tells about a lost sheep and lost coin, and this story is one of three that continue the theme of lostness. The focus here is not on the one who is lost, but on what it means to be found.

22. Le Guin, "Ones Who Walk Away."

CHAPTER 6

1. Plato, *The Apology* 28a–32e.

2. There are many good treatments of the subject, and I would refer the reader to Jersak, *Her Gates Will Never Be Shut*.

3. Bernstein, *Formation of Hell*, 271.

4. Emphasis Rohr's, adapted from Rohr, *Immortal Diamond*, 85–86, 90.

5. Holsten and Traub, dir., *Barefoot Artist*.

6. For a reading that does not depict the Samaritan woman as a "fallen" character, see Brant, *John*, 82–87.

7. Ibid., 84, translates 4:9 as "How is it that you, being a Jew, beg [*aiteis*] [something] to drink from me, a Samaritan woman?"

8. As quoted by Shelly Rambo in "Wounds Surfacing."

9. Calvin, *Commentaries on John*, 20.20.

10. Widdicombe, "Wounds and the Ascended Body."

11. The wounds of Christ "testify to the intimate connection between the economy of God's salvific work within the created order and the eternal economy." Ibid., 137.

12. Because of the limitations of this work and my own expertise on this subject, I would direct the reader to other helpful resources, such as Heath, *Wounds of Sexual Abuse*; and Rambo, *Resurrecting Wounds*.

13. Palmer, "Broken-Open Heart."

14. D. F. Brown, "Bình Định Blues."

CHAPTER 7

1. The alternative title of the film was *The Clansman*. In his 2018 film *BlacKkKlansman*, director Spike Lee depicts the use of this film at a Klan initiation rally to show how it has been used by hate groups to bolster their ideology.

2. Rezayazdi, "Director Nate Parker." One caveat to Parker's statement is that it does not hide his own incriminations regarding rape allegations. It is indeed wearisome that this film attempted to counter Griffith's work, but is also fraught with controversy.

3. Because Plato's student Aristotle also wrote a work by the same name, known as *The Politics*, we inherit the title *The Republic*, derived from the Latin name rather than the Greek.

4. Hebrew avoids some of these problems by using two separate words to express righteousness (*tsaddiq*) and justice (*mispat*), e.g., Amos 5:24. However, these words are often used interchangeably as synonyms. This is a reminder again that every translation of a text is also an interpretation of it.

5. Perkins, *Dream with Me*, 110.

6. Christianity Today editors, "MacArthur's 'Statement on Social Justice.'"

7. MacArthur et al., "Statement on Social Justice."

8. Israel without the Occupied Territories is 8,019 square miles, compared to the 8,729 square miles of New Jersey.

9. Volf, *Exclusion and Embrace*, 227.

10. Following Eugene Boring's interpretation, I would concur that the imagery in the book of Revelation is of figurative and literal violence. It does not attempt to predict the future, but rather to paint a picture (or multiple pictures) of how God has defeated and is defeating the forces of darkness in this world to establish the New Jerusalem that "comes down out of heaven" and onto earth. Boring, *Revelation*, 42.

11. Perez, Morris, and Ellis, "Alleged Santa Fe High School Shooter."

12. Langman, "Bullying and School Shootings."

13. Grabow and Rose, "57 Times as Many School Shootings." It is important to note that the gun violence in Central America can be traced to gang violence and cartels, which ultimately comes back to the demand for drugs in the United States.

14. Other texts, such as the flood narrative and the total destruction of peoples (Hebrew *cherem*), and similar, should be read through the lens of a progressive view of God's revelation and not as a depiction of some Old Testament wrathful God. We only know what we are given in our language, philosophy, culture, and mental capacities at the time. When we were children, we understood God in more simplistic ways; as adults, these notions should change. Similarly, the way earlier peoples understood God is different from how we understand God now. This is just a simple fact of human development.

15. Kornfield, *Art of Forgiveness*, 42.

16. U.S. Department of Justice, "Sentencing Circles."

17. Westervelt, "Alternative to Suspension."

18. Flood, "Substitutionary Atonement," 149. Emphasis in the original.

19. See Miguel A. De La Torre's discussion of forgiveness and repentance in *Embracing Hopelessness*, 111–12.

20. *Trump v. Hawaii*, 585 U.S. ___ (2018) at 38, quoting Robert Jackson's dissent in *Korematsu v. United States*, 323 U.S. 214 (1944) at 248. The 2018 opinion also states,

"The forcible relocation of U.S. citizens to concentration camps, solely and explicitly on the basis of race, is objectively unlawful and outside the scope of Presidential authority."

21. Bulatao and Anderson, eds., *Differences in Health.*

22. Participation rates are higher among people of color, but white people represent the highest number of recipients when measured by race. Government assistance program participation by race in 2015: 35 million white people, 24 million Hispanics and Latinos, and 20 million Black people. Cole, "Surprising Facts about Welfare Recipients."

23. Paul of Tarsus invokes this same imagery of "written on their hearts" when he writes in Romans 10 that "if you confess with your lips that Jesus is Lord and believe in your heart that God raised him from the dead, you will be saved" (v. 9). Here belief is not merely an intellectual exercise, but rather the allowing of an impression to take place, just as a pencil or pen makes an impression on paper. The paper is thus changed.

24. Luke's version of the Lord's Prayer links sins to economic indebtedness. For Luke, being poor and being caught in a cycle of monetary debt is a sin in that it is a burden for the oppressed that requires liberation.

25. Found in the writings of Maximus Confessor (d. 662); Gregory of Nazianzus (d. 389/90).

26. A note on the figures: These images depict the relationship between the persons of God in terms of community. I am not attempting here to illustrate what the Council of Nicaea (325 CE) or the subsequent six other ecumenical councils were seeking to establish in their formulation of the doctrine of the Trinity.

27. Bui, Coates, and Matthay, "Years of Life Lost."

28. Rasmussen, *Earth-Honoring Faith,* 121.

29. Franco and Radford, "Ex-KKK Member Denounces."

30. Ibid.

31. Park, "Minjung Theology," 3.

32. Bonhoeffer, *Letters and Papers from Prison,* 312.

33. Nguyen, *Nothing Ever Dies,* 56.

BIBLIOGRAPHY

Alexander, Michelle. *The New Jim Crow: Mass Incarceration in an Age of Colorblindness*. New York: The New Press, 2012.

Alter, Robert. *Genesis: Translation and Commentary*. New York: W. W. Norton, 1996.

Anselm of Canterbury. *Why God Became Man* [*Cur Deus homo*]. In *Anselm of Canterbury: The Major Works*. Edited by Brian Davies and G. R. Evans. Oxford, UK: Oxford University Press, 1998.

Athanasius. *De incarnatione* [*On the Incarnation*]. In *Athanasius: "Contra gentes" and "De incarnatione."* Edited and translated by Robert W. Thomson. Oxford, UK: Oxford University Press, 1971.

Augustine. *Confessions*. Translated by Henry Chadwick. Oxford, UK: Oxford University Press, 1998.

———. *De Trinitate*. Edited by W. J. Mountain. CCSL 50. Turnhout: Brepols, 1970.

———. Sermon 117. In *Sermones de Scripturis de Novo Testamento*. Vol. 38 in *Patrologia Latina*. Available at http://www.augustinus.it/latino/discorsi/index2.htm.

Aulén, Gustaf. Christus Victor: *An Historical Study of the Three Main Types of the Idea of Atonement*. Translated by A. G. Hebert. New York: Macmillan, 1969. First published 1931.

Bass, Diana Butler. "Table of Gifts." The Work of the People video, 9:40. https://www.theworkofthepeople.com/a-table-of-gifts.

Beilby, James, and Paul R. Eddy, eds. *The Nature of Atonement: Four Views*. Downers Grove, IL: InterVarsity, 2006.

Bernstein, Alan E. *The Formation of Hell: Death and Retribution in the Ancient and Early Christian Worlds*. London: University of London Press, 2003.

Bonhoeffer, Dietrich. *Letters and Papers from Prison*. New York: Touchstone, 1953.

The Book of Common Prayer. New York: Church Publishing, 1979.

Boring, Eugene. *Revelation*. Interpretation: A Bible Commentary for Preaching and Teaching 43. Knoxville, TN: Westminster John Knox, 2011.

Boyle, Gregory. *Barking to the Choir: The Power of Radical Kinship*. New York: Simon and Schuster, 2017.

Brant, Jo-Ann A. *John*. Paideia Commentaries on the New Testament. Grand Rapids, MI: Baker Academic, 2011.

Brown, D. F. "Bình Định Blues." In *Ghost of a Person Passing in Front of the Flag*, 18. Houston, TX: Bloomsday Literary, 2018.

Brueggemann, Walter. "The Liturgy of Abundance, the Myth of Scarcity." *Christian Century*, March 24, 1999. https://www.christiancentury.org/article/2012-01/liturgy-abundance-myth-scarcity.

Bui, Anthony L., Matthew M. Coates, and Ellicott C. Matthay. "Years of Life Lost due to Encounters with Law Enforcement in the USA, 2015–2016." *Journal of Epidemiology and Community Health* 72 (2018): 715–18.

Bulatao, R. A., and N.B. Anderson, eds. *Understanding Racial and Ethnic Differences in Health in Late Life: A Research Agenda*. Washington, DC: National Academies Press, 2004. https://www.ncbi.nlm.nih.gov/books/NBK24685/.

Calarco, Santo. "Punished 'for' or 'by' Our Sins—The Suffering Servant of Isaiah 53." *Clarion Journal of Spirituality and Justice* (October 15, 2013). https://www.clarion-journal.com/clarion_journal_of_spirit/2013/10/punished-for-or-by-our-sins-the-suffering-servant-of-isaiah-53-santo-calarco.html.

Calvin, John. *Commentaries on John*. Vol. 2, translated by William Pringle. Grand Rapids: Christian Classics Ethereal Library, n.d. https://ccel.org/ccel/calvin/calcom35/calcom35.i.html.

———. *Institutes of the Christian Religion*. Translated by Henry Beveridge. Grand Rapids: Christian Classics Ethereal Library, 1845, http://www.ccel.org/ccel/calvin/institutes/.

Christianity Today editors. "John MacArthur's 'Statement on Social Justice' Is Aggravating Evangelicals: Christians Are Talking Past Each Other Once Again. What's Going On?" *Christianity Today*, September 12, 2018. https://www.christianitytoday.com/ct/2018/september-web-only/john-macarthur-statement-social-justice-gospel-thabiti.html.

Clement of Alexandria. *The Stromata*. In *Fathers of the Second Century: Hermas, Tatian, Athenagoras, Theophilus, and Clement of Alexandria*. Vol. 2 of *The Ante-Nicene Fathers*, edited by Philip Schaff. Grand Rapids, MI: Christian Classics Ethereal Library, 2004. http://www.ccel.org/ccel/schaff/anf02.

Cole, Nicki Lisa. "9 Surprising Facts About Welfare Recipients." ThoughtCo, updated September 28, 2019. https://www.thoughtco.com/who-really-receives-welfare-4126592.

Cone, James. *The Cross and the Lynching Tree*. Maryknoll, NY: Orbis, 2011.

Considine, Kevin P. *Salvation for the Sinned-Against: Han and Schillebeeckx in Intercultural Dialogue*. Eugene, OR: Pickwick Publications, 2015.

Davis, James Martin. "Midland Voices: Graveyard in the Clouds." Omaha World-Herald, May 26, 2018. https://www.omaha.com/opinion/midlands-voices-graveyard-in-the-clouds/article_6b0b6b31-33d1-5c8d-994e-16b250be85fc.html.

De La Torre, Miguel A. *Embracing Hopelessness*. Minneapolis: Fortress, 2017.

Dick, Phillip K. *The Man in the High Castle*. New York: G. P. Putnam's Sons, 1962.

Duck, Ruth C. "Hospitality to Victims: A Challenge for Christian Worship." In *The Other Side of Sin: Woundedness from the Perspective of the Sinned-Against*, edited by

Andrew Sung Park and Susan L. Nelson, 165–180. Albany: State University of New York Press, 2001.

Ekblad, Bob. "God Is Not to Blame: The Servant's Atoning Suffering according to the LXX of Isaiah 53." In *Stricken by God? Nonviolent Identification and the Victory of Christ*, edited by Brad Jersak and Michael Hardin, 180–204. Abbotsford, BC: Fresh Wind Press, 2007.

———. *Reading the Bible with the Damned*. Louisville, KY: Westminster John Knox, 2005.

Emerson, Michael. *Market Cities, People Cities: The Shape of Our Urban Future*. New York: NYU Press, 2018.

———. and Christian Smith. *Divided by Faith: Evangelical Religion and the Problem of Race in America*. New York: Oxford University Press, 2001.

Federal Bureau of Investigations. "2017 Hate Crime Statistics: Incidents and Offenses." FBI, accessed January 4, 2020, https://ucr.fbi.gov/hate-crime/2017/topic-pages/incidents-and-offenses.

Flood, Derek. "Substitutionary Atonement and the Church Fathers: A Reply to the Authors of *Pierced for Our Transgressions*." *Evangelical Quarterly* 82, no. 2 (2010): 142–159.

Franco, Aaron, and Morgan Radford. "Ex-KKK Member Denounces Hate Groups One Year after Rallying in Charlottesville." NBC News, August 9, 2018. https://www.nbcnews.com/news/us-news/ex-kkk-member-denounces-hate-groups-one-year-after-rallying-n899326.

Girard, René. *The Scapegoat*. Baltimore: The Johns Hopkins University Press, 1986. Originally published as *Le Bouc émissaire*. Paris: Grasset, 1982.

Gohringer, Jeff. "The Cost of the Crisis." Better Markets, July 20, 2015. https://bettermarkets.com/newsroom/better-markets-releases-cost-crisis-report-detailing-how-financial-crash-will-cost.

Gorringe, Timothy. *God's Just Vengeance: Crime, Violence and the Rhetoric of Salvation*. Cambridge, UK: Cambridge University Press, 1996.

Grabow, Chip, and Lisa Rose. "The US Has Had 57 Times as Many School Shootings as the Other Major Industrialized Nations Combined." CNN, May 21, 2018. https://www.cnn.com/2018/05/21/us/school-shooting-us-versus-world-trnd/index.html.

Graves, Anthony. *Infinite Hope: How Wrongful Conviction, Solitary Confinement, and 12 Years on Death Row Failed to Kill My Soul*. Boston: Beacon Press, 2018.

Gregory of Nazianzus. "Ep. 101 (To Cledonius)." In *Cyril of Jerusalem, Gregory Nazianzen*. Vol. 7 of *The Nicene and Post-Nicene Fathers*, Series 2, edited by Philip Schaff. Grand Rapids, MI: Eerdmans, 2007.

Hạnh, Thích Nhất. *Living Buddha, Living Christ*. New York: Riverhead, 1997.

Hannam, James. *The Genesis of Science: How the Christian Middle Ages Launched the Scientific Revolution*. Washington, DC: Regnery Publishing, 2011.

Hardin, Michael. "Christianity Is Changing," Patheos, September 2014. https://www.patheos.com/blogs/christianityischanging/2014/09/the-eucharist-4/.

Harper, Lisa Sharon. *The Very Good Gospel: How Everything Wrong Can Be Made Right*. Colorado Springs, CO: WaterBrook Press, 2016.

Heath, Elaine A. *Healing the Wounds of Sexual Abuse: Reading the Bible with Survivors*. Ada, MI: Brazos Press, 2019.

Holsten, Glenn, and Daniel Traub. *The Barefoot Artist*. New York: Film Movement, 2014. 83 minutes.

Ignatius. *The Epistle of Ignatius to the Smyrnaeans.* Page 297 in *Clement. II Clement. Ignatius. Polycarp. Didache.* Vol. 1 of *The Apostolic Fathers*, edited and translated by Bart D. Ehrman. Cambridge, MA: Harvard University Press, 2003.

Irenaeus. *Against Heresies.* In *The Apostolic Fathers with Justin Martyr and Irenaeus*, edited by Philip Schaff. Grand Rapids, MI: Eerdmans, 2001. Originally published as *Libros quinque adversus haereses.* Edited by W. Wigan Harvey. Cambridge, UK: Typis Academicis, 1857.

Jersak, Bradley. *Her Gates Will Never Be Shut: Hope, Hell, and the New Jerusalem.* Eugene, OR: Wipf and Stock, 2009.

———. *A More Christlike God: A More Beautiful Gospel.* Pasadena, CA: CWRpress, 2015.

Jersak, Brad, and Michael Hardin, eds. *Stricken by God? Nonviolent Identification and the Victory of Christ.* Abbotsford, BC: Fresh Wind Press, 2007.

Jones, Camara. "Allegories on Race and Racism." Filmed July 10, 2014, in Atlanta, GA. TEDxEmory video, 20:43. https://youtu.be/GNhcY6fTyBM.

Kendi, Ibram X. *How to Be an Antiracist.* Rev. ed. New York: One World, 2019.

———. "What's the Difference Between a Frat and a Gang?" *The Atlantic*, March 20, 2018." https://www.theatlantic.com/politics/archive/2018/03/america-frats-and-gangs/555896/.

Kornfield, Jack. *The Art of Forgiveness, Lovingkindness, and Peace.* New York: Bantam, 2002.

Langman, Peter. "Statistics on Bullying and School Shootings." School Shooters, November 2014. https://schoolshooters.info/sites/default/files/bullying_school_shootings_1.1.pdf.

Lee, Jasmine C., and Haeyoun Park. "15 Black Lives Ended in Confrontations with Police. 3 Officers Convicted." *New York Times*, updated October 5, 2018, https://www.nytimes.com/interactive/2017/05/17/us/black-deaths-police.html.

Le Guin, Ursula K. "The Ones Who Walk Away from Omelas." In *New Dimensions 3.* Edited by Robert Silverberg. Garden City, NY: Nelson Doubleday, 1973.

Lonergan, Bernard. *Philosophical and Theological Papers 1958–1964.* Vol. 6 of *Collected Works of Bernard Lonergan*, edited by Robert Croken, Frederick E. Crowe, and Robert M. Doran. Toronto: University of Toronto Press, 1995.

MacArthur, John, et al. "The Statement on Social Justice and the Gospel." 2019. https://statementonsocialjustice.com.

MacIntyre, Alasdair. *Dependent Rational Animals: Why Human Beings Need the Virtues.* Rev. ed. Chicago: Open Court, 2001.

———. *Whose Justice? Which Rationality?* Notre Dame, IN: University of Notre Dame Press, 1988.

Madoff, Bernard. "Bernard L. Madoff's Statement to the Court." *New York Times*, June 29, 2009. https://www.nytimes.com/2009/06/30/business/30bernietext.html.

Martin, Michel. "Slave Bible from the 1800s Omitted Key Passages That Could Incite Rebellion." *All Things Considered*, December 9, 2018. https://www.npr.org/2018/12/09/674995075/slave-bible-from-the-1800s-omitted-key-passages-that-could-incite-rebellion.

Middleton, J. Richard. *The Liberating Image: The* Imago Dei *in Genesis 1.* Grand Rapids: MI, Brazos Press, 2005.

Moltmann, Jürgen. *The Crucified God: The Cross of Christ as the Foundation and Criticism of Christian Theology.* Minneapolis: Fortress, 1993.

National Center for Chronic Disease Prevention and Health Promotion (US) Office on Smoking and Health. *The Health Consequences of Smoking—50 Years of Progress: A Report of the Surgeon General.* Atlanta, GA: CDC, 2014. https://www.ncbi.nlm.nih.gov/books/NBK294310.

Nguyen, Viet Thanh. *Nothing Ever Dies: Vietnam and the Memory of War.* Cambridge, MA: Harvard University Press, 2011.

Nietzsche, Friedrich. On *the Genealogy of Morals.* Translated by Walter Kaufmann and R. J. Hollingdale. New York: Vintage Press, 1989.

Nouwen, Henri. *The Return of the Prodigal Son: A Story of Homecoming.* New York: Doubleday, 1992.

Origen of Alexandria. *Origen: Contra Celsum.* Translated by Henry Chadwick. Cambridge, UK: Cambridge University Press, 1980.

Palmer, Parker. "The Broken-Open Heart: Living with Faith and Hope in the Tragic Gap." Reprinted from *Weavings: A Journal of the Christian Spiritual Life*, vol. 24, no. 2. (March/April 2009). https://www.couragerenewal.org/PDFs/PJP-WeavingsArticle-Broken-OpenHeart.pdf.

Park, Andrew Sung. "Minjung Theology: A Korean Contextual Theology," *Indian Journal of Theology* 33, no. 4 (October–December 1984).

———.The Bible and *Han.*" In *The Other Side of Sin: Woundedness from the Perspective of the Sinned-Against*, edited by Andrew Sung Park and Susan L. Nelson, 45–59. Albany: State University of New York Press, 2001.

———. *Racial Conflict and Healing: An Asian American Theological Perspective.* Eugene, OR: Wipf and Stock, 2009.

———. *The Triune Atonement: Christ's Healing for Sinners, Victims, and the Whole of Creation.* Louisville, KY: Westminster John Knox, 2014.

Pelagius. *To Demetrias.* In *Pelagius: Life and Letters.* Translated by B. R. Rees. Suffolk, UK: Boydell Press, 1998.

Percival, Henry R., ed. *The Seven Ecumenical Councils.* Vol 14 of *Nicene and Post-Nicene Fathers*, Series 2, edited by Philip Schaff and Henry Wace. Peabody, MA: Hendrickson, 1995.

Perez, Evan, Jason Morris, and Ralph Ellis. "What We Know about Dimitrios Pagourtzis, the Alleged Santa Fe High School Shooter." CNN, May 21, 2018. https://www.cnn.com/2018/05/18/us/dimitrios-pagourtzis-santa-fe-suspect/index.html.

Perkins, John M. *Dream with Me: Race, Love, and the Struggle We Must Win.* Grand Rapids, MI: Baker Books, 2017.

Piper, John. "Is God Less Glorious Because He Ordained That Evil Be?" Desiring God, July 1, 1998. https://www.desiringgod.org/messages/is-god-less-glorious-because-he-ordained-that-evil-be.

Plato. *Plato: Complete Works*, edited by John M. Cooper. Indianapolis: Hackett, 1997.

Rambo, Shelly. *Resurrecting Wounds: Living in the Afterlife of Trauma.* Waco, TX: Baylor University Press, 2017.

———. "Wounds Surfacing." Stanley Grenz Lecture Series, Seattle, WA, November 2015. https://vimeo.com/146464773.

Rape, Abuse, and Incest National Network. "Campus Sexual Violence: Statistics." RAINN. Accessed January 8, 2020. https://www.rainn.org/statistics/campus-sexual-violence.

Rasmussen, Larry. *Earth-Honoring Faith: Religious Ethics in a New Key.* New York: Oxford University Press, 2013.

Rezayazdi, Soheil. "Five Questions with *The Birth of a Nation* Director Nate Parker." *Filmmaker Magazine*, January 25, 2016. https://filmmakermagazine. com/97103-five-questions-with-the-birth-of-a-nation-director-nate-parker/.

Richards, E. Randolph, and Brandon J. O'Brien, *Misreading Scripture with Western Eyes: Removing Cultural Blinders to Better Understand the Bible*. Downers Grove, IL: IVP Books, 2012.

Rohr, Richard. *Immortal Diamond: The Search for Our True Self*. San Francisco: Jossey-Bass, 2013.

Ross, Ellen M. *The Grief of God: Images of the Suffering God in Late Medieval England*. Oxford: Oxford University Press, 1997.

Ross, Virginia, and William DeJong. "Other Drug Use and Abuse on Campus: The Scope of the Problem." U.S. Department of Education, April 2009. https://files.eric .ed.gov/fulltext/ED537628.pdf.

Shermer, Michael. "The Number of Americans with No Religious Affiliation Is Rising." *Scientific American*, April 1, 2018. https://www.scientificamerican.com/article/ the-number-of-americans-with-no-religious-affiliation-is-rising/.

Somashekhar, Sandhya. "The Disturbing Reason Some African American Patients May Be Undertreated for Pain." *Washington Post*, April 4, 2016. https://www.washington post.com/news/to-your-health/wp/2016/04/04/do-blacks-feel-less-pain-than-whites-their-doctors-may-think-so/.

Steenberg, M. C. *Of God and Man*. London: T&T Clark, 2009.

Thomas Aquinas. *Summa theologiae*. Translated by Fathers of the English Dominican Province. Notre Dame, IN: English Classics, 1947.

Tidball, Derek, David Hilborn, and Justin Thacker, eds. *The Atonement Debate: Papers from the London Symposium on the Theology of Atonement*. Grand Rapids, MI: Zondervan Academic, 2008.

U.S. Census Bureau. "About Race." U.S. Census, last revised January 23, 2018. https:// www.census.gov/topics/population/race/about.html.

U.S. Department of Justice. "Sentencing Circles." n.d. http://www.courts.ca.gov/ documents/SentencingCircles.pdf.

Volf, Miroslav. *Exclusion and Embrace: A Theological Exploration of Identity, Otherness, and Reconciliation*. Nashville: Abingdon, 1996.

Wallis, Jim. *America's Original Sin: Racism, White Privilege, and the Bridge to a New America*. Grand Rapids, MI: Brazos Press, 2017.

Weaver, J. Denny. *The Nonviolent Atonement*. Rev. 2nd ed. Grand Rapids, MI: Eerdmans, 2011.

Westervelt, Eric. "An Alternative to Suspension and Expulsion: 'Circle Up!'" NPR, December 17, 2014. https://www.npr.org/sections/ed/2014/12/17/347383068/ an-alternative-to-suspension-and-expulsion-circle-up.

Widdicombe, Peter. "The Wounds and the Ascended Body: The Marks of Crucifixion in the Glorified Christ from Justin Martyr to John Calvin." *Laval théologique et philosophique* 59, no. 1 (February 2003): 137–54.

Williams, James G. *The Bible, Violence, and the Sacred: Liberation from the Myth of Sanctioned Violence*. New York: HarperCollins, 1995.

Williams, Reggie L. *Bonhoeffer's Black Jesus: Harlem Renaissance Theology and an Ethic of Resistance*. Waco, TX: Baylor University Press, 2014.

Wink, Walter. *The Powers That Be: Theology for a New Millennium*. New York: Doubleday, 1998.

THE AUTHOR

Phuc Luu (福刘) immigrated with his family to the United States from Vietnam when he was four. Luu is now a theologian, philosopher, and artist creating work in Houston, Texas, to narrow the divide between ideas and beauty. If theology is speaking about God, Luu seeks to give new language and grammar to what theology has not yet said. He served for seven years on the Nobel Peace Prize Committee for the American Friends Service Committee (Quakers). He holds degrees in theology (MDiv, PhD) and philosophy (MA), but has learned the most from the places where people ask difficult questions, where they live in the land between pain and hope, and where these stories are told.